A Day of Rest

D1304513

A Day of Rest

Creating
a Spiritual Space
in Your Week

Martha Whitmore Hickman

AVON BOOKS NEW YORK

Pages 131–132 constitute an extension of this copyright page.

AVON BOOKS, INC.
1350 Avenue of the Americas
New York, New York 10019

Copyright © 1999 by Martha Whitmore Hickman
Front cover illustration by Anton Stetzko
Inside cover author photograph by Peter Hickman
Interior design by Kellan Peck
Published by arrangement with the author
ISBN: 0-380-79727-5
www.avonbooks.com

Library of Congress Cataloging in Publication Data:

Hickman, Martha Whitmore, 1925-
  A day of rest : creating a spiritual space in your week / Martha
Whitmore Hickman
     p. cm.
1. Sabbath. I. Title.
BV125 .H53 1999   98-54742
263' .2   dc21   CIP

First Avon Books Trade Paperback Printing: March 1999

AVON TRADEMARK REG. U.S. PAT. OFF. AND IN OTHER COUNTRIES, MARCA
REGISTRADA, HECHO EN U.S.A.

Printed in the U.S.A.

OPM   10   9   8   7   6   5   4   3   2   1

To Mary, Esther, and Stephen, beloved sisters and brother,
who shared my childhood sabbaths

Acknowledgments

My thanks go to Ann McKay Thoroman of Avon Books, who suggested this project to me and guided me through it with imagination and admirable flexibility; to my agent, Harvey Klinger, for his good-humored encouragement and elan; to the members of my Tuesday-evening writing group, who attend to one another's work with almost as much care as to their own; to the trustees and staff of the Ragdale Foundation, for the gift of time and attendant TLC; and to my husband, Hoyt, for helping find the right books to read, for sharing the wealth of his knowledge and experience, and for the enduring pleasure of his company.

Contents

—✺

wordswithoutspacemakenosense
wordswithout space makenosense
words without space make no sense

lifewithoutspacemakesnosense
lifewithout space makesnosense
life without space makes no sense

remember the sabbath

—✺

GEORGE WHITE

I go among trees and sit still.
All my stirring becomes quiet
around me like circles of water.
My tasks lie in their places
where I left them, asleep like cattle.

Then what is afraid of me comes
and lives a while in my sight.
What it fears in me leaves me,
and the fear of me leaves it.
It sings, and I hear its song.

Then what I am afraid of comes.
I live for a while in its sight.
What I fear in it leaves it,
and the fear of it leaves me.
It sings, and I hear its song.

After days of labor,
mute in my consternations,
I hear my song at last,
and I sing it. As we sing
the day turns, the trees move.

WENDELL BERRY

~⟲

CHAPTER ONE

What's Wrong with This Picture?

A woman writes in a national magazine of driving across the George Washington Bridge and suddenly being inundated by a flood of tears. The stress of making adequate day care arrangements for her children and transportation arrangements to get them back and forth to school and hiring extra help to fill in the gaps of time when neither the day care provider nor she nor her husband can be with them overshadows the satisfaction and joy she should be taking in a life that is rich and full.

A psychiatrist suggests that the reason so many people are on drugs to treat psychoneurotic disorders is that we are too busy, our plates are too full.

A friend says in frustration, "I'm busier now than I was when we had four kids at home—and I'm angry most of the time."

The chief of the women's health programs at Harvard Medical School's Division of Behavioral Medicine and Mind/Body Medical Institute says stress is the leading health problem facing American women.

An economist reports that work hours and stress are

up and sleep and family time are down for all classes of employed Americans.

A spokeswoman for a leading fashion designer says of prospective customers, "Their lives are so hectic. They're getting children ready for school, going to work, picking up the kids, getting dinner made, participating in social events in the evening. What women really want is clothes that make life easier." Her prescription? "A medium-thigh-length dress in a bright floral print. Throw a jacket over it, and head for the office; tie a sweater 'round your shoulders and take the kids out for a movie. Pair the dress with pearls and sexy slingback heels, and evening wear is a cinch. You could literally go from a picnic to a formal restaurant with one great dress." To which my reaction is, *Oh, sure.* But at least she's got the situation right.

A National Commission on Civic Renewal has been established to try to find out why Americans are "so cynical, so distraught, so angry, so ticked off about so many things"—a condition alluded to by one member of the commission as "grumpiness. . . . Some of the grumpiness has to do with the dislocations of the Information Age— not being able to work the VCR, having to change jobs every five years. But more of it comes from the conditions of our family like not being able to take walks after dark and worry about educational standards." A columnist, commenting on the nearly one million dollars awarded this commission, says, "Professional worry about America's soul has become a national pastime."

And all the time we are being bombarded with messages to acquire more goods (including labor-saving devices and elaborate exercise equipment), take advantage of special money-saving offers for exotic trips, invest in— and learn to use—more sophisticated electronic equipment to put us in touch with more people and more information than we can possibly assimilate.

We are so used to a constant barrage of stimulus that sometimes we seem to have lost all impulse for quiet. There are people who turn on the television as soon as they wake up and leave it on all day. We retract from such mindlessness. But when was the last time any of us got in the car and did *not* turn on the radio, let alone that device hazardous to the human ear—the cellular telephone? A writer, in commenting on the changes the electronic age has brought, suggests that with the barrage of competing stimuli we are in danger of losing our sense of self. "And our collective sense of absence, of homelessness, being cut off from something vital, will grow stronger too."

It isn't only the adults among us who are besieged with too much stimulus, too much to do. Children are programmed into extra courses in gymnastics, languages, music, swimming, karate, science—until they run out of days in the week. These are all valuable in themselves, but where is the leisure of mind to daydream, to dawdle, to wonder "What am I going to do?" When I observe the frenzied pace of many children's lives today, I recall the time my young son, who obviously valued his leisure hours highly, upon being told he'd been invited to a birthday party the

One of the main causes of modern stress is that we have too much to do. Consequently, Sabbath days—when we don't have to do anything—can release us from the anxiety that accompanies our work. . . . Our false need to be productive (even in the church) builds stress, especially when we find ourselves unable to meet our exorbitant expectations. We scramble after the security of personal status and think that we will be invincible when we have climbed the corporate ladder and demanded human respect—only to discover our perpetual vulnerability.

MARVA DAWN

following Saturday, said ruefully, "I hate to spoil Saturday with a birthday party." That was the old birthday party. Today's birthday parties are extravaganzas at entertainment complexes, with catered refreshments and programmed games and enough stimulus to last a month. (To be sure, such an arrangement does save busy parents time and stress involved in doing all that at home—and cleaning up after it!)

Certainly, overload is not everyone's problem. There are probably people who suffer from understimulation, or at least from lack of inner resources to know what to do with long stretches of time. I remember thinking, back in the dim past before "everyone" had television, what a source of refreshment and interest television could be for the aged or ill and how pleased we all were when my mother and father—on the edge of frailty—gave in and bought their first TV set. But if we think of most adult Americans still in the full flush of activity, we would find many more yearning for quiet spaces in their lives than for more activities to fill up empty hours.

And some people have little choice in regard to overcrowding their lives. Some need to work two jobs to support themselves and their dependents. Some jobs require almost a constant presence—though we would look a long time before we found in today's society acceptance of Andrew Carnegie's demands of his steel mill workers that they work twelve hours a day, seven days a week.

But for the vast majority of us, we do have some power over our schedules and the degree of busyness we take on. Still, we search for ways to deal with the psychic and physical overload that defines us. With our lives that should be brimming with meaning and satisfaction, we are hungry for a peace we know must be out there, or in there—but we don't seem able to avail ourselves of its healing and refreshment.

So we work at having "quality time," and we wonder what is the absolute minimum we need to exercise to keep our hearts in good running order (twenty minutes three times a week), and hope that tomorrow—or next week—or next month—the commotion will ease.

Recognition of the problems of overload has been with us for a number of years. Transcendental Meditation, the Relaxation Response, and other techniques have helped many distraught people recover some sense of perspective—and improve their health. Retreat centers are springing up all over the country—places where people can get away for a day or a week to be able to "recollect in tranquillity" who they are and what they are about.

In Kentucky the Abbey of Gethsemani (made famous by Thomas Merton), which accepts outside visitors for five-day Monday-through-Friday retreats or weekend respites, is booked for months in advance. A friend takes a week of her precious annual vacation to go to a retreat center where she can read, think, sit in stillness, walk in stillness, be with a resident guide for a period of each day. Then and only then does she feel refreshed and ready to embark on the rest of her vacation—a trip with a friend through scenic New England. Some retreat centers

My guess is that many . . . would welcome an alternative way between our overaccommodation to the culture and sectarian or inappropriate withdrawal from it. This alternative involves the integrity of a particular way of life that is tested by scriptures, tradition, and the fresh movement of the Holy Spirit through our time. It will take many forms, depending on our different life circumstances. In this sense each of us is an experiment, a unique person in a unique community at a unique time, pioneering a way of life.

TILDEN EDWARDS

do offer the services of a "spiritual director" to guide the solitary retreatant through the shoals of silence: If you're used to round-the-clock busyness, long stretches of silence can be frightening.

The tranquillity achieved in such experiences is a precious gift—but soon we are back in the frazzle again, and the mind keeps whirring and, even in moments of respite, can't stop. I remember stepping onto a moving treadmill that was going faster than my steps could keep up with, and my feeling of panic that I was going to fall flat on my face—or even worse, so disorienting was the experience—before I scrambled to get off the device, and *then* learned how to turn it off.

Is it worse than it used to be—this sense of rushing through life pell-mell—or of standing dazed in the middle of the road while life rushes by on both sides? Are we just dragging our feet and protesting because change is so threatening? Certainly the advent of the microchip has changed the *technicalities* of modern life. What does it mean that I can fax messages within minutes to my niece in Indonesia? Or that I can become chummy with strangers across the nation through chat rooms on the Internet? Change the technicalities enough and you change the central perceptions of what life is about.

Somewhere along the line, according to some analysts, we have moved from being a society of people whose lives are based on the givenness of the communities in which we find ourselves—family, religious community, civic unit—to a society of individuals, defining ourselves by what we produce and what we consume—which leads to all kinds of frenetic striving: If I have no community to help give my life meaning, I have the impossible task of trying to make my mark in life *by myself*.

If I *can* make these transglobal communications, does it mean I *should*? If the technology is there and I don't use it, will I be a misfit in my own society? If I do, I add a whole constellation of potential frustrations (as well as some benefits) to my life. But when do I have the leisure to really look at these questions, let alone decide what to do about them?

So I may swing from avid attention to my work—or guilty neglect of it—to some necessary but sometimes stupefying relief from such a pace and mood, and then back again, and wonder if I have been reading the wrong clues, or when things are going to "settle down" so I can catch my breath.

We are often a distraught people, wishing for a more pervasive peace, a way of structuring our lives so they don't echo the title of a play of some years back, *Stop the World I Want to Get Off!* What are we to do?

The rhythm of life for countless people, set up by this culturally pressured way, thus emerges as one that oscillates between driven achievement (both on and off the job) and some form of mind-numbing private escape. This crazed rhythm, based on a distorted view of human reality, increasingly poisons our institutions, relationships, and quality of life.

TILDEN EDWARDS

The intent of this book is to help us—by stories, examples, suggestions—to avail ourselves of some of the power and life found in the ancient Judeo-Christian—and to some extent Muslim—concept of Sabbath: that ancient programmed rhythm of life designed to keep us steady in the midstream of life without the constant danger of being swept off our feet. Where did it come from? What is its nature, its call to us? How does it feed our hunger? How can it redeem our lives today?

⁓

CHAPTER TWO

A Brief History of the Seven-Day Week

" *See* you next week." "Two weeks vacation." "Once a week." "A week at a time."

What is this phenomenon—the week? Who—or what—ordained that we should divide our long stream of time into these units of seven twenty-four-hour cycles, each with its own agenda, its own emotional tone, often its own foods or its own way of dressing? We have come to rely so heavily on the week to mark our time in manageable segments that it is almost hard to imagine how disoriented we would be if we didn't have this tidy unit of measurement. Robinson Crusoe, alone on his island and realizing he is losing his sense of time, begins to mark notches in a piece of wood—six shorter notches, and one long, six short, one long—a week.

Seven. Is there something mystical about the number seven? If Snow White had had five dwarves—or ten, would the story have worked as well? Jacob, one of the early patriarchs of Judaism, worked seven years for the hand of Rachel, the bride of his choice, and then, hoodwinked into accepting her older sister, Leah, worked another seven to claim Rachel as his own. "Seven years of plenty and seven years of famine," Joseph predicts for the Egyptian pharaoh. "How often should I forgive? As many as seven times?" Peter asks Jesus. "Not seven times, but seventy times seven," Jesus replies. "Come seven, come eleven," goes the dice thrower's chant.

Virtually alone among the designations by which we mark our tenure on the planet, the concept of "week" has no echo in nature. The twenty-four-hour cycle of day and night reflects the rotation of the Earth toward and away from the sun. The months correspond roughly to the waxings and wanings of the moon. The passage of a year marks the time it takes for the Earth to travel around the sun. But the week?

The fact that the week has no obvious corollary in nature represents one of humanity's successful efforts to free itself from the dictates of nature: We are not totally bound by the travels of the moon or the rotation of the Earth.

Then where did it come from, if not from nature—this social construct based on mathematical repetition, this convenient way of grouping our lives into manageable units that have their own pattern of rise and fall—what one writer has called "the beat" of the week? Some speculate that a regular week became necessary when a market economy developed to the point that a predictable market day became necessary.

It wasn't always a seven-day week. The ancient Egyptians were the first to establish a continuous weekly cycle separate from any of the cycles of nature. Their weeks were ten days long, and three of them made up a thirty-day month. (The complexities of trying to make a recurrent calendar that fits with what we do know about the workings of the Earth and the solar system are hinted at in the conundrum faced by anyone trying to understand leap years, months of different lengths, etc.)

No one knows exactly how the concept of the seven-day week first came into being, but it has evolved over time from two different sources, each independent of the other. The first, and by far the older source, is the creation account of the Old Testament in which God created the world in six days and then rested on the seventh. "And on the seventh day God finished the work that he had done, and he rested on the seventh day from all the work that he had done" (Genesis 2:2).

This pattern is reinforced by the fourth of the commandments God gave Moses on Mount Sinai, which again describes the pattern and also admonishes the Hebrews to follow this pattern in their own lives: "Remember the Sabbath day, and keep it holy. Six days you shall labor and do all your work. But the seventh day is a Sabbath to the Lord your God; you shall not do any work—you, your son or your daughter, your male or female slave, your live-stock or the alien resident in your towns. For in six days the Lord made heaven and earth, the sea, and all that is in them, but rested the seventh day; therefore the Lord blessed the Sabbath day and consecrated it" (Exodus 20:8–11).

This has been the pattern of Jewish culture from earliest times, and it is on this pattern—of six days and then rest—that Christian and Muslim and secular society have formed our common life.

Far from the Judean hills, and at a much later time, the seven-day week also evolved in the Hellenistic world. Ancient astronomers, peering at the night sky, observed that there were seven heavenly bodies that *seemed* to move: Saturn, the sun, the moon, Mars, Mercury, Jupiter, and Venus. We can only conjecture as to how this observation moved into adopting a recurring pattern of seven days. One writer suggests that adopting the concept of recurring time, of a cycle of time, is a comforting security—a stay against what could be terror if one thinks of time as infinitely passing, as linear only. The Earth and the heavens do reinforce the notion of recurring time, and there were the seven so-called "planets." It is hard to imagine the confusion and lostness that could occur if we had no way of dividing time into manageable blocks—bigger than a day, smaller than a month. The skies suggest the number seven. A week, maybe? For whatever combination of reasons—astronomical, astrological, mathematical—this perception of a recurring weekly cycle based on the seven "planets" occurred in the Hellenistic world around the end of the second century B.C.E.

The two ancient cultures with their concept of a seven-day week—the Jewish, based on the Old Testament creation account, and the Hellenistic, based on the astrological heritage of Egypt, Babylon, and Greece—came together about the time Christianity, with its origins in Judaism and *its* week, was being introduced into the Roman Empire. Though by the end of the first century Rome did not yet have an official week, unofficially, along with the lands bordering the Mediterranean, it had adopted the recurrent cycle of seven days as a measurement of time. The days of the week kept their planetary designations—Sunday (the day of the sun), Monday (the day of the moon), Tuesday (the day of Mars), Wednesday (the day of Mercury), Thursday (the day of Jupiter), Friday (the day of Venus) and Saturday (the day of Saturn)—became established as standard. (The English names for the days Tuesday, Wednesday, Thursday, and Friday were derived from the names of the corresponding Norse gods.)

The distinctive feature of the Jewish week—six days of work and then a day of rest, which was not necessarily part of the "planetary" week—has greatly affected religious and cultural life ever since its inception. The day of rest—the Sabbath—is the hinge on which the week turns, the distinctive day that marks the end of one week and the beginning of the next unit of time, as though a long rope were knotted at stated intervals and one measured the rope by counting the succession of knots. Six days, and then a day of rest.

> The ancient Romans had two categories, a *dies festus*, a holy day, and a *dies profestus*, the ordinary working day.
> Hallowed time stood apart. . . .
> The people who celebrated were taken out of ordinary time. They were restored to it in improved condition.
>
> GERALD SLOYAN

The rest day may have shifted, or expanded, but the concept has stayed with us. That it has persisted through so many generations of recorded history speaks not only to our reverence for and honoring of the story but that it must also in some way fit our own psychic and physical needs at a profound level. Studies done at the University of Arizona showed a biological need for rest every seventh day and the energizing value of rest: "Failure to rest after six days of steady work will lead to insomnia or sleepiness, hormonal imbalances, fatigue, irritability, organ stress, and other increasingly serious physical and mental symptoms." There seems to be some evidence that the human biological clock runs on a twenty-five-hour cycle. But because by the structures of society, we can't get up an hour later each day. The body needs a period of time to catch up. We can believe it. Work six days, then rest.

Rest was much more than sitting down and admiring the sunset—or one's handiwork. "Rest" meant a change of pace, observations of faith in home and temple as well as cutting back work to only what was necessary to keep the wheels of life turning.

The early Christians, many of whom had been Jews, continued to honor the concept of observing Sab-

> The Sabbath is not for the sake of the weekdays; the weekdays are for the sake of Sabbath. It is not an interlude but the climax of living.
>
> ABRAHAM JOSHUA HESCHEL

bath on Saturday—or from sundown on Friday to sundown on Saturday. That was their own heritage, too. Many of the noted events in Jesus' life took place on the Sabbath. He began and closed his ministry on the Sabbath. But over time the day *after* Sabbath, what came to be known as "the Lord's day" or, in Quaker tradition, as "First Day," became the focus of the community's gathering together. Why? It was on the first day of the week that Christ had been raised from the dead. It was Sunday, on the day of Pentecost, that the Holy Spirit appeared, "like the sound of a mighty wind." It was on Sunday, the first day of the week, that God separated the light from the darkness.

But Sunday was a workday in first-century Rome. So the Christians would gather before dawn, when work began, or after work was ended, and celebrate their commemorative Eucharist and share an agape meal.

In 321 the Emperor Constantine, who later became a Christian, declared that on Sunday his soldiers should have a day of rest and recreation, that the law courts and shops should be closed and townsfolk should stop work. Later in that same century, under Emperor Theodosius I, public entertainments on Sunday were prohibited, as well as all but essential employment. Gradually, Christians moved away from traditional Sabbath observance and took Sunday as their day for worship and for rest. The Jewish community, of course, continued, as much as it was able, to observe its own pattern of Sabbath keeping.

So now we have Saturday—or, more particularly from sundown on Friday to sundown on Saturday—as the holy day, the Shabbat, for Jews, and Sunday as the holy day, the Sabbath, for Christians—though Seventh-Day Baptists and Seventh-Day Adventists have considered the commandment to observe the Sabbath as the holy day binding. Most churches take this commandment to be not a moral law but as part of the ceremonial rite of the Jews.

The choice of Sunday is accurate as far as the Christian story goes (the day of Christ's resurrection—"the first day of the week"), but something of the specialness of the Jewish Sabbath adheres to its contiguous day, Sunday. Would it "work" as well if Tuesday, say, were the holy day for Christians? We are too formed by our habit of observing Sunday as "the Lord's Day" to know, but somehow it seems unlikely.

The words: "On the *seventh day* God *finished* his work" (Genesis 2:2; italics added by author) seem to be a puzzle. Is it not said: "He *rested* on the *seventh day* . . . In *six days* the Lord made heaven and earth" (Exodus 20:11; italics added by author)? We would surely expect the Bible to tell us that on the sixth day God finished His work. Obviously, the ancient rabbis concluded, there was an act of creation on the seventh day. Just as heaven and earth were created in six days, *menuha* was created on the Sabbath.

"After six days of creation—what did the universe still lack? *Menuha*. Came the Sabbath, came *menuha*, and the universe was complete." . . .

"What was created on the seventh day? *Tranquility, serenity, peace, and repose.*"

ABRAHAM JOSHUA HESCHEL

Mohammed recognized the value for Jews and Christians of having a gathering for worship every seven days and wanted also a special day on which Muslims can gather for community prayer. Not the Jewish Sabbath, surely, or the Christian "Lord's Day"—they were already taken. But maybe to cluster with them, to choose Friday? For whatever collection of reasons (including celebrating the creation of Adam) it is Friday that is the chosen day for Islam for the community to gather. These three major faiths, which have much in common as well as much to distinguish them, "rub shoulders," figuratively speaking, on their chosen holy days. The fact that each of these three major faiths recognizes the importance of a special day, a day set apart, may say something to all of us, followers or observers, about the importance of Sabbath.

There were some interesting departures from the seven-day-week scheme, and it may be worthwhile to look at them briefly.

Because a chief function of the seven-day week was to enrich religious experience with a climactic day for gathered worship, any attempt to undermine religious expression might well attack the patterns of work and worship. And so they did. An effort was made during the French Revolution to replace the seven-day week with a ten-day week—the acknowledged aim of which was "To abolish Sunday." From 1793–1805 the *decade*, as it was known, was the ruling calendar, but it failed absolutely in its intention and the seven-day week was restored.

An even more radical attempt to destroy the seven-day week was made in the Soviet Union in 1929, where, in an attempt to secularize the population, the state introduced a continuous workweek with different parts of the workforce having differing five-day cycles of work and rest. A husband might have Tuesday as his day off while his wife might have Thursday. With this staggered pattern of work it was difficult indeed to gather religious communities or protesting groups of workers at manageable times. This experiment also failed, and the seven-day week was restored in 1940.

There have been other esoteric shifts in the concept of a week—a nineteen-day week known to the Bahá'i faith, a Nigerian four-day market week, a Javanese six-day *sadwara*, a Mayan twenty-day week. These variations demonstrate the maneuverability of this kind of unit of time measurement—no ascending or descending moon, no advance of winter weather or summer heat to argue with the human construct dividing the days.

These variations, bizarre as they seem, may have more in common with our current experience than we recognize. A person on kidney dialysis surely marks the days of the week differently. A three-day span? A four-day span? People who work "flextime" are able to manipulate their week to suit their needs and lifestyles. Four workdays of ten hours each are giving people a full "week's worth" of work in scarcely more than half the days of the week. A schoolteacher's week is surely different in October than in July. Medical residents on call, airline pilots on reserve, farmers whose work is subject to the caprices of weather—all have weeks shaped by unforeseeable events. A seven-day week is still the "norm" for these people, but often it is observed from afar. Honoring the Sabbath may be a catch-as-catch-can affair.

There are also many people for whom the week's balance shifts because Sabbath work goes with their vocational territory. Clergy, obviously, are in this group, as are any others vocationally connected to churches or temples—music directors, cantors, church custodians; many restaurant workers and, since commerce has taken over much of our Sunday quiet, workers in grocery and department stores are also in this group. Machines have to be kept running. Firemen are on duty, as are police, and personnel in institutions caring for people around the clock. Some other provision needs to be found for them if they are to have the refreshment the Sabbath offers.

Over the years we have seen the steady erosion of traditional Sabbath observances. But the rhythm of the week and the weekend, the continuing marking of time by the seven-day week, appear in no jeopardy at all. Time stretches ahead of us in these wonderful "medium-sized" units—a week. And then another week. A new chance to succeed. A new chance to fail. A new chance to work. A new chance to rest. A new chance to return to our communities, or to stay away from them. And then the weekend is past. A new workweek is about to begin.

~

CHAPTER THREE

The Rhythm of the Workweek

$\mathcal{W}$hat is the shape and tenor of the days that make up the usual workweek? If we need respite and recharging on our Sabbath—whether Saturday or Sunday or Friday—with what baggage from the workweek do we head into the Sabbath?

A couple of acknowledgments before we begin: For many people the usual five-day workweek is known by its absence rather than its presence. For parents of young children—particularly if one of the parents is a stay-home care giver—there is no such thing as a Monday-to-Friday workweek. "Do you work?" we ask young parents, implying that being at home with young children is a kind of ongoing holiday. Parents may even fall into the same trap. "When I was working," I hear myself saying, referring both to a time before child rearing and a time after, during periods of which I was gainfully employed—at a workplace other than my writing desk.

A second acknowledgment. As suggested in the last chapter, for many people their workweek regardless of family responsibilities bears little resemblance to this

Monday-to-Friday pattern. People have to work on weekends, are "on call" for emergencies, must respond to the vagaries of weather, and for any number of reasons may have an atypical work schedule.

For many of us the five-day workweek is a fairly modern institution. In my childhood my father, a lawyer, always worked Saturday morning. For him and for many others at that time, the "weekend" began on Saturday noon. But when we think of the usual workweek in the United States we think of Monday through Friday.

Part of the shape and tenor of the week will depend on the communities of which we're a part. A man who lived for four years on the campus of Notre Dame University described the ritual building of energy and anticipation during the football season: Monday through Wednesday there would be intense speculation about the game. On Thursday the alumni and families and friends of students would start arriving. On Friday the bookstore would do a land-office business selling college T-shirts and mugs. And then on Saturday—the climactic event of the week—The Game! Presumably Sunday, in addition to whatever else, was a day of appraisal and shared experiences of The Game. And then it was Monday again.

Monday. Take Monday. The day of the moon. *You* take Monday? Blue Monday, when reputedly more suicides are committed than any other day, more patients admitted to emergency rooms, more people call in sick at work. It doesn't stop there. A study of retired men, reported in *Prime Health and Fitness* magazine, found that the majority of deadly arrhythmias—dangerous irregular heartbeats—occurred on Mondays. The chief of cardiology speculated, "This may be due to a memory of what Monday meant to them when they were working."

"Monday, Monday, don't trust that day," goes the song of a few years back. My husband, as a child of seven, wrote in his first-ever diary the single cryptic sentence for a long-ago April 15, "I did not like it because it was Monday." Monday—washday? It used to be, when I was growing up in Massachusetts. I wonder whether part of the rationale for Monday washday was to start out with a clean slate, or maybe that doing laundry was a relatively routine task and could be accomplished with something less than full vigor and imagination.

> You get the Monday you deserve from the Sunday you've spent.
>
> CIFERNI

At least on Monday you know where you are—the day after the weekend. "Did you have a nice weekend?" we ask each other, hopefully, perhaps nostalgically, as we go into the office on Monday morning. When I was dating, staying out late on weekends, Monday was the day, while going about my work in probably desultory fashion, for assessing how the relationship was going after another weekend of spending time together. The glow—or shadow—of the weekend often lies over this first workday of the new week, at least until we get ourselves in gear and can proceed with moderate efficiency and attention to the tasks at hand.

Perhaps as a way to offset this tendency to be less than avid about work, some businesses schedule very important meetings on Mondays—as if plunging into the cold water of Monday will wake you up. I understand that some publishing houses schedule regular editorial meetings on Mondays. As a writer I wonder whether they would accept more—or fewer—or different manuscripts for publication if the meetings were on Wednesday, say, or on Friday?

By Monday afternoon (unless we are too tired to be

fully conscious) we are getting into the swing of things again, and by evening it may be as though the weekend never happened. The church I belong to has its church council meetings on Monday evenings. Are we by then beginning to pick up some momentum? I hope so.

There is, of course, another way of looking at Monday. Monday does promise a whole new span of workdays to accomplish desired goals—a fresh start. A friend tells me that as a child she loved Monday because it meant going back to school. And for people who are uneasy with the unscheduled time of the weekend, or who are perhaps lonely for the community the workplace offers, the return to schedules may be a welcome shift.

Folklore offers its own descriptions of the day: "Solomon Grundy, Born on Monday," goes the old nursery rhyme, beginning the unfortunately rapid life of one whose health began to deteriorate on Thursday, culminating in his death on Saturday and burial on Sunday, "And that was the end of Solomon Grundy." "Monday's child is fair of face," starts the poem describing the distinctive qualities of children born on each of the days of the week. A plus for Monday—not to be taken lightly for one born on Wednesday. More on that later.

By Monday evening we are probably all tired out from this day of transition—back into the routine of the week's work patterns. Probably no particular drive to go out tonight. Just as well. The movie theaters are open, but often the live theaters are closed on Mondays, as are many museums. Monday, then, is a day to recoup from the weekend as well as a day to begin to accrue substance to the week, as tumbleweed gathers more of itself unto itself as it rolls along the ground, or a snowball gathers snow as it rolls down a hill. We have four more days before a major shift in mood, but there will be slighter shifts along the way. We've made it through so far.

Tuesday, the day of the planet Mars, the god of war, translated somewhere along the line to more closely resemble the Nordic name, Tyr. "Tuesday's child is full of grace," the poem goes, hopefully bearing little resemblance to the aforesaid god. And as for Solomon Grundy, he was "Christened on Tuesday," moving through his life cycle with appropriate speed. Tuesday. The second day of the workweek. In the days before wash 'n' wear, Tuesday was the day to do the ironing. Does Tuesday seem a little nondescript—a minor caesura in the week's passage? Or maybe a second chance at a new beginning? We are on the rising arc of this five-day span; hopes for accomplishment this week may still be high. My own experience of Tuesday is conditioned by my membership in a writers' group that for more than fifteen years has met every Tuesday evening, to listen to one another's work and generally to shore one another up. There is still time in the week to utilize the energy and ideas we get from being together.

"I did not pay much heed to Wednesday," my husband wrote as a child in his diary. It is an easy day to slide past, right in the middle of the workweek, the school week, halfway to the weekend and the Sabbath. The day of the planet Mercury, the name taken from the Norse name of the god, Woden, chief god of the pagan Anglo-Saxons. There are events that accrue to Wednesday. Some churches have midweek services on Wednesday evening and choir practice is often on Wednesday. There are apt to be matinees of live theater in the big cities. A notable day for Solomon Grundy, who was "Married on Wednesday." A notable day for me, who was born on Wednesday and who as a child minded, really *minded*, that in the old nursery rhyme the line for Wednesday reads, "Wednesday's child is full of woe," especially as my sister, fifteen months my senior, was born on Sunday—the designation for which is, "But the child who is born on the Sabbath day shall be happy and good and wise and gay." We are the best of friends, which shows that the day of the week is not everything.

Thursday. The day of the planet Jupiter. Named from the Norse name, Thor. God of the heavens, sometimes referred to as the god of thunder, rain, and farming. We're getting toward Friday now. Newscasters are predicting the weekend weather—not only for farmers but for the rest of us. The weekend food specials are advertised in the paper—time to write out the shopping list. Notices for weekend yard sales appear. It's a day to make a last push before the workweek tapers off. Did you get done what you wanted? There's still tomorrow. After that, unless you're a workaholic or yield to outside pressure you'll probably wait until Monday to start it all up again. Thursday is a bad day for Solomon Grundy, who "Took ill on Thursday," and if you were born on Thursday you have "far to go," which could be good or bad, depending on departure point and destination. As for my husband's childhood diary, the entry is, "It was nearly Friday."

And then it *is* Friday. The day of Venus, named for the Norse god, Freya, in Teutonic mythology the goddess of love, beauty, and fecundity. A fitting tone for the weekend? Freya comes from the same root as the Old English word, free. We can feel it coming. We are tired, ready for a break. We begin to feel the closing down early in the day. Jews, if they can, prepare for the start of Sabbath at sunset. Some businesses close at noon on Friday, particularly during the summer months. Even when regular hours are kept, the clearing of the desks, the watering of the plants, have a special aspect of closure today. We talk about weekend plans, wish each other a good weekend, and leave, grateful for the breather. The culture waits for us. TGIF (thank God it's friday) goes the old slogan— an acronym adopted as the name of a well-known restaurant chain. The restaurants and lounges will be full this evening. The movies change— maybe go to a new movie? Go out together as a family? Eat a celebrative meal at home? Maybe watch *Washington Week in Review* and *Wall Street Week*. Born on Friday? "Friday's child is loving and giving." Solomon Grundy, "Worse on Friday," hastens toward his demise.

But where did the week go? At the moment we don't care. The arc of the workweek, which peaked on Wednesday, has slid along its downward thrust. We're ready for a change, for some refreshment of body and soul. It's time to relax into the weekend, time to anticipate the Sabbath. The single sentence in the diary? "We looked forward to Saturday."

Holiness and balance don't necessarily come to mind when life is overflowing with demands and the sink is full of dishes. But when you can strike a personal balance in the midst of these, you catch a glimmer that holiness is here, too. "In the mud and scum of things," wrote Emerson, "always, something sings."

VICTORIA MORAN

CHAPTER FOUR

The Weekend: the "Other" Day

Leisure does not just happen; it has to be
thought out beforehand.

GERALD SLOYAN

*W*hether you work a traditional work week, work at
home, or stay home to care for young children,
for many people the weekend is probably a two-day
blur—or a two-and-a-half-day blur if we consider the
weekend as starting on Friday afternoon. Many people
may make no distinction between the day on which religious observance traditionally takes place and the other,
the "free" day. But whether or not we observe a Sabbath,
the cultural imprint of each of these weekend days is different.

The culture is admittedly prejudicial on behalf of
those who observe Sunday as their Sabbath. In most settings, Jewish merchants would be at a severe disadvan-
tage if they closed their stores on Saturday. Muslims, who
have their gathering for worship on Friday, must also
work around customs that decree Friday as a business
day. And for more subtle reasons than the opening or
closing of business establishments, the ballast of the
weekend shifts depending whether the "free" day, the
"other" day, comes before the Sabbath, or after it. Are we

getting ready for the big day, or are we winding down in the wake of our day of Sabbath observance?

For most of American culture, including my own tradition, the Sabbath is on Sunday, so Saturday is the "other" day of the weekend. Saturday. The seventh day of the week, named for the Roman god, Saturn, and for the planet of the same name. The free day—free for catching up, for shopping, for doing household chores—putting on the screens, mowing the lawn, putting a new filter in the furnace, getting haircuts. A good day for soccer, baseball, roller skating on the sidewalk, for picnics in the park. Maybe some family outing or "night on the town." It's a relatively quiet day in hospitals: Everyone who can go home has gone, and unless it's an emergency, new admissions wait until Monday. Saturday and Sunday have the lowest rates for suicide.

Perhaps the illusion of holiday lowers our guard. It's also the day when more alcohol is consumed, which may have something to do with its being the day with the highest number of homicides and of deaths due to motor vehicle accidents. The 1973 mass firings in the Nixon entourage seemed more abrupt and ominous because they occurred on Saturday—"the Saturday night massacre." It was on a Saturday night in 1981 that the Polish government crushed the Solidarity movement.

In ancient astrology there were negative associations with the planet Saturn. The word "saturnine" means "having a gloomy temperament." On the other hand, and more congruent with our preferred ambiance for this day, is the word Saturnalia, for the ancient Roman festival, "a time of general feasting and unrestrained merrymaking." The prime night for dating. But what if you don't have a date? "Saturday night is the loneliest night," the song goes.

Of all the days, this "free" day of the weekend probably allows individuals and families the most latitude of all on how they spend the day. But free or not, creatures of habit that we are, we probably develop our own patterns (rituals if you will) for this day, too. Is that a matter of efficiency, or would we otherwise feel at loose ends, either because our identity is so bound up with our work that we are lost without it, or because we are just uneasy without a schedule to shape our days?

When I was growing up, Saturday had its own climate—special projects, a household-oriented island of getting ready, before we plunged into the next week, starting with Sunday and then the weekdays of work and school. Often my mother would bake bread—a process that went on throughout much of the day, its intervals as reliable as the Catholic Observance of the Hours or the Muslim calls to prayer. First the mixing—yeast afloat on warm water, add milk, flour, salt, turn the kneading hook, stopping to add more flour "until you can poke a finger in and it comes out dry."

When my brother got old enough to have substantial muscle power in his arms, she would call him (in those prefeminist days) to "come and turn the handle," and he would come and turn the black knob of the bread hook arm while mother and sisters looked on appreciatively. Then she'd set the covered pail on a board on the radiator for a couple of hours while the dough accomplished its first rising.

When the bread was sufficiently risen, she'd dump it out on a floured board and knead it, lifting, folding, pressing with the heels of her hands. "See those bubbles?" my mother would ask, pointing to small blisters in the creamy dough. "You knead until those are all gone." Cut it into three mounds—shape the two large mounds into loaves and the small one into a dozen rolls, to fit in the round pan. Let them rise again, then bake—the smell the fragrance of incense—turn them out on racks to cool, their upturned crusts grainy and golden.

My mother would incline her head for the sniff test—"You know by the smell when they're done." Butter knives in hand, we'd gather at the kitchen counter and as soon as the rolls were cool enough to handle, we'd each break one off, lay a slender slice of butter against it—the butter would melt immediately—and eat. Two rolls was the suggested limit—"Save some for supper." The bread of life, and never a religious feast observed with more delight.

Against this tapestry of bread making would go the other rituals of Saturday. Other cooking, perhaps—homemade applesauce to be pressed through the food mill, Boston baked beans simmering in the oven, removed long enough for the bread to bake, then put back in. Maybe a cake or some homemade ice cream for Sunday. A heartier than usual lunch—ready for when my father came home from his morning's work at the office. In the afternoon perhaps a trip to the grocery store, or to the shoe store for school shoes.

My father had his own Saturday afternoon agenda—change into khaki pants and work in the garden or yard—in baseball season coming in periodically to turn on the radio and learn how the Red Sox were doing, maybe complete some minor household repairs.

Supper (a New England designation for the evening meal) was often baked beans, cabbage salad, applesauce, more of the wonderful rolls—and, redundant though it may seem, a roll of steamed New England brown bread, cut in slices and served on the plate, along with the beans, by my father. His own preference was to put the beans *on* the brown bread; the rest of us liked them on the side. Should we have a guest, my father would ask, as regularly as any catechetical question, as he held the spoonful of beans low over the brown bread, "On? Or off?" I think he lived in hope that one of us—or at least a guest whose preference was heretofore unknown—would join his camp, and if such a guest was found, he would go on in his wry sardonic way to compliment said guest on such good judgment.

Then Saturday night baths. Maybe a family game of Michigan. And then to bed. The next day was Sunday.

There were departures from this, of course. During the course of my growing up my sister and I took several series of Saturday-morning art classes at the local art center—the class membership drawn from all over the city and presenting us with a more heterogeneous group of peers—one of whom, many years later as a university graduate student, remet my sister. They were married some months later. I'm sure the Saturday-morning art class in common wasn't the decisive compatibility, but it didn't hurt, either.

As I got older, Saturday held adventures for me, too: going with a girlfriend to a local swim club where the swimming was secondary to the social exchanges—or silences—with the newly interesting crop of adolescent boys. Saturday was the free day. You never knew quite how it would turn out.

Today's Saturday rituals are surely different. In families, if both parents—or a single parent—are working out-

side the home, and particularly if a person or family observe one day of the weekend as a Sabbath, major chunks
of the free day may well go to maintainance chores—grocery shopping, cleaning, errands. The chores a stay-at-
home parent could get out of the way by the weekend are
still there staring an employed person in the face when,
tired from the week's work and frazzled with everything
needing to be done, such a person moves into the day.
Family outings, if they are possible, must be fit in with
other things. Maybe one reason so many teenagers go to
the mall is "there's nobody to play with" at home.

The mall has become a ritual for our time—not just
on the weekend but maybe particularly then. When I happen to be in a mall on a Saturday, I invariably see many
clusters of young families—a father pushing an infant in a
stroller, a mother and an older child clearly in tow. They
may have bags shoved into the carrying basket behind the
baby, but they are clearly there on an outing, strolling in
leisurely fashion, taking in the sounds and sights—maybe
a modern-day version of a day in the park or a ride in the
country. It's harder and harder to find pleasant roads to
drive on in the country. It's even harder to find the country!

By Saturday evening the crowds are thinning out (unless there's a movie complex), and there's probably somewhere better to go. A party? A quiet evening at home?
Finishing up the Saturday tasks in preparation for the Sabbath? Some churches are holding Saturday evening services. A place to go on Saturday night. A way to fulfill an
obligation so you have the whole of Sunday off. Different
patterns for different times.

In all this shifting of locales and commitments, do we
sometimes wonder, as we come to the end of the day,

whether we are making the right choices? We who, at the push of the button on the bread machine, can accomplish—and with a wonderful fragrance, too—what my mother gave hours of her Saturday to do? We can buy pre-washed salad greens in resealable bags and with the help of power tools can cut our lawns and trim our hedges in a fraction of the time these things used to take. Yet we seem busier than ever.

> The solution of mankind's most vexing problems will not be found in renouncing technical civilization, but in maintaining some degree of independence of it.
>
> ABRAHAM JOSHUA HESCHEL

Casting back over the last hundred years, we know how the workweek has, at least for many, shrunk from seven days to six to five and a half to five. We have, in the ensuing freedom, more options for uses of time than our ancestors dreamed of. Are we using that freedom well? The workdays—Monday through Friday—may be pretty well prescribed for us. But today and tomorrow are more within our control. This "free" day is a day on the calendar to play with, a day to get ready for, or remember, our Sabbath—in church, in temple, at home, in the restorative places of our lives.

> It was said of him [the desert father, Abba Arsenius (360–440)] that on Saturday evenings, preparing for the glory of Sunday, he would turn his back on the sun and stretch out his hands in prayer toward the heavens, till once again the sun shone on his face. Then he would sit down.
>
> BENEDICTA WARD

Even now, I wake up on Saturday morning with a different feel than on other days. A holiday from my work. Even doing the wash seems pleasantly mindless. Tomorrow our schedule is pretty well set. But today—what shall we do today? It is open season, a good anticipation of tomorrow. The pleasure of deciding, among a few "givens" like watering the plants, doing the wash, what we'll do with our "free day." Saturday is a catch-up day. But we might want to go to a movie. Or walk around the lake. "Saturday's child must work for a living," the rhyme goes. But it doesn't feel like that today.

And tomorrow? The Sabbath. We have waited for it in longing. "O day of rest and gladness," the old song begins.

Is it?

CHAPTER FIVE

The Sabbath: Where Did It Go?

$\mathcal{W}$ hat happened to the time-honored custom of observing a day of rest, a day of Sabbath, as all but essential to personal and community well-being?

There are many reasons—some of them referred to earlier—but let's take another look. We can list some of them almost as easily as we can say the alphabet. Maybe a brief look at them will help us find our way back.

Commercialism of the Sabbath. Jews, other than in Israel, have had to cope with this for a long time. Saturday has always been difficult for Jewish merchants to observe as Sabbath, and when stores first began to remain open on Friday evenings, attendance at Friday synagogue services plummeted. Now Christians who observe Sunday as Sabbath are in a similar bind as more and more stores are open on Sunday. Some do stay closed on Sunday morning. But competition is ever sharpening its claws, and the hour creeps back: Open at 12:30. Open at 11:00. Open at 10:30. Many drugstores and major grocery stores are open twenty-four hours a day, as well as the "mom and pop" stores and the convenience store chains, whose survival is in jeopardy, now that the major grocery stores are open around the clock.

American pluralism. It is widely recognized that if ever we were, we certainly are not now a "Christian nation," with a common pattern of workdays and Sabbath and stated religious holidays. Obviously everyone can't observe everyone's religious holidays (though that would have much to be said for it and is the custom in Indonesia), so we let it go at observing a few national holidays and, for the most part, Christmas. Other faiths and cultures must accommodate their celebrations to what's possible in commercially driven America. The fact that there are more and more mixed marriages, with differing customs, further blurs the lines between traditional Sabbath time and work time for individual families and lends sanction to the opportunism of commercial interests. And admittedly, with so many people working full time—or having two or three jobs—doing major shopping on the Sabbath is an easy pattern to fall into.

The mobility of America. Young people who, while they were in their communities of origin, were more likely to adhere to the family and religious traditions, are apt to leave some of that tradition behind when moving to a new location.

Rise of individualism as opposed to identifying with a common life beyond the self. All of us are members of a number of communities: the community of the family, our work community, our neighborhood, perhaps a faith community, a community based on common leisure interests. But in some ways we have become a nation of loners, looking for self-actualization, self-fulfillment. There is even a magazine called *Self!* This has its positive aspects, but it can lead to a privatization mentality, in which we protect ourselves, ostrichlike, against the problems and needs of others and, as a by-product, against common sources for renewal.

The shifting balance between work and home. With more and more families being two-career families, a lot of the energy and emotional investment and sense of accomplishment gravitates toward work. Work can be a more comfortable environment than home. A mother of six says, "I work in the library so I can see I've got something done!" Another mother says, "Vacation for me is when the children are in day care." Aside from comfort there is the fear that, unless one is working constantly, one cannot build a career, afford a home, send the children to college. Such anxieties may be well-founded, but the lines between work and home become increasingly fluid. People bring their work home, with home computers wired into office computers. Where is the will and definition to carve a day of rest in such a scheme?

Past and current excesses which give the whole religious enterprise a bad name. This goes back a long time! In the book of Acts (Acts 20:7–12) there's an account of Paul's preaching so far into the night that a young man was overcome by heat and fatigue and fell from an upper story to the courtyard below. A modern-day counterpart is told of a boy who, seeing a memorial plaque on the sanctuary wall, asked his father what it was about. "That's to honor the people who died in the service," the father said, to which the child replied, "Was it the first service or the second service?"

To this sense of mild unease about the use of a day (too-long services, a general sense of malaise and prohibition), we can add the truly destructive uses of religious feeling—as in Waco, the Jim Jones massacre, the bizarre tragedy of Heaven's Gate. Or the less lethal but also offensive maneuverings of television evangelists who exploit people's wish for God for their own ends.

Overprogramming of the Sabbath. One facet of this is the plethora of sports events—some of them brutal and fiercely competitive—that belie the nature of Sabbath rest and seem to focus the attention of much of the nation, not for the pleasure of watching athletes exhibit superb bodily skill, but for the benefit of corporations who pay millions of dollars for a few minutes of advertising time.

> Almost everyone has a mental image of spending all day in a churchy way which will simply spread the pall of mass or Sunday service over twenty-four hours, thus destroying a perfectly usable day.
>
> GERALD SLOYAN

The overprogramming extends to our personal—and community—lives. Some of this is with the best of intentions. Good causes require meetings. Sunday is a free day. Why not bring a sandwich and stay on after church or temple service—we can probably get through the necessssary business quickly? There are compassionate concerns that are honored by Sabbath attention—taking flowers, or food, or communion, or just our company, to the sick and elderly. There are meetings traditionally held in the afternoon or evening—youth groups, for example—which are a source of refreshment and fun and deepening community. But others are expediencies—we need to schedule a meeting and there is the stretch of time and *voila!* Almost without realizing what we're doing, we've made the Sabbath as cluttered with business as any other day.

Our fear of unstructured time. If I am not working, who am I? If I have free time, will my demons return—those thoughts and fears and possibilities I am able to sidestep by keeping busy. Will I feel useless, uneasy? Will something *new* be expected of me?

Reading down this list—and one could surely add other reasons for the demise of Sabbath freedom, Sabbath rest—the heart sinks. *Honor* the Sabbath? We do well to survive it!

But wait. Throw the baby out with the bathwater? Not on your life.

A few moments of reflection, and most of us would readily agree that we are hungry and thirsty for the breather, the profound calm, the sense of being in touch with our deepest reality, that the Sabbath offers.

Churches must be careful . . . not to devour Sabbath freedom with "religious" or charitable obligations. Filling Sunday afternoons with church committee meetings, for example, is a terrible violation of this freedom.

DOROTHY BASS

But not so fast. The bad news is that the necessary retrofitting of our lives will take some work and a lot of resolve, and probably some trial and error.

The good news is we don't have to invent anything or exhaust ourselves chasing an elusive goal. The Sabbath is already there, waiting for us to enter its portals, sit down, take a deep breath, and look around.

CHAPTER SIX

Reclaiming the Sabbath: How to Make It Happen

*O*ur "how to" is shaped by what we want when we open our hands and hearts and minds to receive the gifts of Sabbath. Do we want to be playful, boisterous even? Do we want quiet? To stay home? Attend a religious service? Go somewhere else special—a park? A concert? Do we want solitude, or to be with friends? Eat simply, or have festive food? Perform some act of service? Do we want a day with planned activities? Time free to follow our own impulses? Maybe all of the above in infinitely variable combinations—a "movable feast"?

Let's assume for the purposes of this chapter that you are a person for whom attendance at religious services is part of your Sabbath observance. Each of us has a variety of reasons for wanting to observe the Sabbath in this way. Some have been referred to in previous chapters, but here is a quick rundown of possible "Reasons Why I Go to Church—or Temple—or Mosque."

To strengthen bonds with communities of church, temple, or mosque.

To share with other members of the community in worship and in commitment to service.

To enlarge a sense of "family," to whom as persons in need we can turn and be assured of welcome.

To obey the biblical commands.

To honor the histories of the faith and of the saints and pilgrims;

Worship and remember
to keep the sabbath day.
Take a rest and think of God.
Put your work away.

NATALIE SLEETH

to have a sense of the religious community as going back through history as a sustaining, enabling reality to which we now belong.

To share with other people the sense of transcendence, of the reality of God as a Being who is present in the world, who takes us to heart, cares for us, loves us, and guides us.

To savor "the beauty of holiness" in temple, church, or mosque.

To get a sense of order and comfort in a chaotic and dangerous world. (Houses of worship are full after disaster.)

You can probably add others.

Or maybe you don't go but you're at least thinking about it—starting, or returning. Maybe you've been wanting to but have been putting it off—I'm already too busy. It's too big a commitment. Sunday is the only free day I have.

Probably true, and true again—that you are too busy. And if you decide to make attendance at services a habit—yes, it is a big commitment. And Sunday may well be the only free day you have. But maybe there are ways you could give attendance at Sabbath services a thoughtful try. As one example—many Christian churches, realizing the need for flexibility and still staying within the traditional understanding of Sabbath as beginning at sundown on Saturday, are now holding Saturday evening services as well as services on Sunday morning.

The quality of the day we honor is surely affected by its context in the rest of the week. For Jews, getting ready for Sabbath usually takes place in the midst of finishing out a week at work. For Christians, there is usually all of Saturday to create a launching pad for the Sabbath. For Muslims in non-Muslim countries, the Sabbath may be no more than an extended lunch hour in the midst of a busy workday. But for whatever use we can make of them, here are some suggestions—many of which could help make of any Sabbath an oasis of rest and regeneration, whether or not one attends religious services.

Clearing the decks. This old nautical term is an apt metaphor for getting ready to receive the Sabbath. With so many people having offices in their homes, this may be especially important. Working at home, we're deprived of the key in the lock or the clanging of the elevator on Friday afternoon to force us to leave the office behind. So, if you work from a home office, tidy up the desk—put away the current project, put the pens and pencils in their receptacles, close down the computer. Take care of personal errands, too—the reminder to the repairman, alerts for the meeting at church next Wednesday, the call to the cat-

> Making of Sunday the community at its best—in church and throughout the day—inspires us to build up that community during the week. Making Sunday a truly prayer-and-rest-filled day could be one of the most prophetic and countercultural moves we could make in these days.
>
> CIFERNI

alog's 800 number even though it advertises "round the clock" service. If these things weigh heavy on your mind and you can't get them done, make a "Things to Do" list for next week and *then* try to dismiss them.

Clearing the decks may mean getting regular household tasks out of the way.

Cook in advance. It has long been the custom in traditionally religious families—and prescribed in the Old Testament—to do none but the most unavoidable meal preparation on the Sabbath. Before the Sabbath, in anticipation of the celebration, wonderful sights and smells may fill the kitchen. When the Sabbath begins, we enjoy the fruits of our labor, but the labor itself is past. Whatever our tradition, and whether we're feeding ourselves, or our family, or hosting a party, we can do as much of the preparation as possible ahead of time. This is the occasion for good use of freezers and convenience foods, as long as they're nutritious and pleasing to look at. I recall the Christmastime when we had sixteen people with us for several days. I had planned and cooked with sufficient advance foresight that it was almost easier than feeding our family of five—as mealtime approaches, look at the list and get the food out of the freezer. Whether food is planned in advance or put together on the spot, the Sabbath is the last of all times to aim at "keeping up with the Joneses." To present guests with simple food—and perhaps to tell them why—is to share the Sabbath message of freedom and simplicity, along with Sabbath hospitality.

Other ways of getting ready? Having the washing and cleaning out of the way. And the clothes ready—casual or more dressed-up—so one doesn't have to churn frantically around looking for the matching belt or a new shoelace. Even the Sunday offering can be put in an envelope and laid out the night before. And the plants can be watered so, refreshed, they, too, can rest in the safety of having what they need.

Getting the family ready. The family will soon enough catch on to the rhythms of Sabbath preparation. I recall the infinite coziness of winter Saturday evenings when I was a child. Often we would have had our baths before supper, even our hair wrapped in curlers for the night, and then supper, in the warmth of our pajamas and robes, maybe a game of dominoes by the fireplace with my grandfather before going to bed. Later, not old enough to date, I recall pressing my Sunday dress on Saturday night while listening to *Your Hit Parade* and the yearning cries elicited by the young Frank Sinatra. Getting ready for Sunday. Much later, as the mother of young children and the wife of a minister, I remember "staying out of his way" while he put the finishing touches on his preparations and doing my own preparations, checking that the children's clothes, and my own, were in order for the next day.

It all depends on us.

Sunday can be nothing:
hours that merely divide
the times that really count

from one another;
space that is useful
only because it groups in sixes
the days of our achievement.

ROBERT HOVDA

Now, many years later, my Sabbath preparations are briefer and more casual. I do make sure the wash is done and put away, that the house is as clean as it needs to be— the degree of need determined by whether we plan any guests during the weekend. One of my departures from my New England heritage is to wash, not on Monday, but on Saturday—which, along with Sunday, is my own personally decreed "time off" from the writing which, now that my children are grown, has become my vocation.

So, with whatever degree of readiness, we enter the

Sabbath. The Jewish Sabbath begins at sundown on Friday and extends until sundown on Saturday. Most commonly, Christians consider their Sabbath to be the full hours of Sunday. But some Christians like to consider Saturday evening as getting-ready time. If Saturday tasks extend into the evening, perhaps Sabbath observance can begin at bedtime on Saturday night with a simple ritual of lighting a candle and offering a prayer of Sabbath welcome.

Establishing the family rituals. The Sabbath arrives. Breakfast first? Or no breakfast? One of the rules (now greatly modified) for Catholics was not to eat before mass. A Catholic friend reminds me, "That's why so many Catholic weddings were in the morning." If breakfast, a special breakfast?

Then getting dressed—probably a time of some flurry, particularly if there are young children involved. It may even develop its own rituals. When our sons were young, getting dressed in "Sunday suits" was in itself an event. Their custom was to turn on the radio to a program with drum rolls and dramatic music; men whose lives had been redeemed from alcohol and a life on the streets told their stories. Our sons became expert at parodying these accounts, occasionally falling on one bed or another, giving outcries of surrender and redemption before completing the dressing tasks and going off in good spirits to Sunday school. They were pushing at the edge of adolescence back then, and I have thought that were there rebellious inner voices suggesting they might rather stay home and why did they have to go—was it because their father was the minister?—the small act of defiance in parodying the dramatic circus they perceived this radio program to be may have spared us all some grief.

My own memories of getting ready for church as a child are of putting on a pretty dress and "Sunday shoes" and of my mother tying ribbons into my hair.

Today the whole thing is a much simpler matter. Our children are long gone from our home and our city. The congregation my husband and I belong to now leans heavily toward the casual side in the matter of Sunday-morning dress. There will be more jeans than Sunday dresses or Sunday suits, and hardly anyone but a visitor would wear a hat. I don't regret this change in custom— though I *like* dressing up. I even remember with pleasure wearing hats. But I keep my sense of "dressing up for church" by wearing perfume. And not just any perfume— of which I have an assortment—but Yardley's English Lavender, my mother's favorite. If it is true, as some suggest, that our sense of smell is the most evocative of all our senses, it is my way of taking my mother's presence with me. And not only her presence, but that of my English grandmother whose name I bear, who came to this country as a young woman. We carry our associations with us. So the place to which I go is not only the beloved congregation to which I have belonged for twenty-five years, but also the church I grew up in. And drifting in the wake of the churches I have attended is the whole community of church—or synagogue, or mosque—the multitude of believers whom no one can number, back to the Greeks who looked up at the sky and wondered whether those heavenly bodies were gods—and back to the patriarch Moses standing barefoot on Mount Sinai while the mountain thundered—and back to Egyptians who thought, indeed, there might be one god—and back to the cave dwellers mixing powdered clay and indigo root and marking stone walls with their own version of I AM against the unknown darkness. All cultures, all times, have groped in art and word and ritual to posit answers to the great questions of meaning—or lack of it—in the universe. So, we go to church.

But in what mind-set? We will consider later some ways of developing a Sabbath frame of mind, but here let us simply acknowledge that if we carry with us into Sabbath services the same "get done and get out" mentality that accompanies much of our weekday activity, any service may seem too long, even tedious— one more thing to accomplish and make some kind of tenuous contact with God. We need to come in a receptive mood, give ourselves over to the mystery around which a worship service dances, trying in images and memories and intuitions to celebrate

Sabbath is a gift you give yourself. If you have a Jewish or Christian background, remember that even God rested: you can, too . . . I know this is difficult to do if you work long hours and you have only two days in the week for marketing and laundry and errands and housework. But devoting a day to your faith and yourself and your family is a magical expenditure that, like tithing your time, will return to you in inexplicable ways.

VICTORIA MORAN

the God who is always in our midst. Someone has said, "We don't go to church. We enter into a worship experience."

Maybe you've been away from—or never been a part of—a worshiping community and are considering entering, or re-entering such a community. Most cities or towns of any size offer what can be a bewildering array of choices. The city of Nashville has six mosques, five synagogues, and almost eight hundred churches! If you are looking for a worshiping community, you will probably choose something compatible with your family's tradition and culture. But narrowing the choices beyond that may take some time and experimenting. Reading the church notes in the newspaper may tell you some of the subtler things you'd like to know—what other activities beside weekly services different congregations are involved in. Worship communities differ in style as well as in theology—within denominations as well as among the major religions. Protestant worship services alone go all the way from Quakers whose services are marked by silent reflection, to services of some of the more "ecstatic" forms of worship during which people engage in spirit-directed shouting, dancing, and falling to the floor. Not all of these are to everyone's taste, but unless health and safety are adversely affected (as in snake handling or witholding health measures from children), people are wisely reluctant to interfere with others' religious practice. The story is told of an Orthodox Jew who refused to sign a neighborhood petition protesting that some noisy pentecostal services were disturbing the peace by saying, "If I thought my Messiah had come I'd sing and dance and shout, and nobody could stop me."

Knowing the range of religious practice may provoke us to examine and better appreciate our own. Particularly if you've been away from the faith, it's a good idea to learn or relearn about the symbols and acts of worship used— the meanings of holy communion in Christianity, the sanctity of Torah in Judaism, the image of the Kaba in Mecca, toward which Muslims face when praying. Study guides for understanding these symbols and acts of worship are readily available. The leader of a worshiping community would probably be overjoyed if you asked him or her to recommend such a guide!

The continuum of widely practiced worship patterns

is long. Some have prescribed forms of worship rituals; others are more spontaneous. Most include periods of reflection on our own needs and the needs of others, sharing of community stories and concerns, addresses to God in worship and petition, and celebration of the community and our life in God.

Celebration is, in some ways, at the heart of it all. In a book called *Why Not Celebrate?*, Sara Wenger Shenk writes, "Celebration is the honoring of that which we hold most dear. Celebration is delighting in that which tells us who we are. Celebration is taking the time to cherish each other. Celebration is returning with open arms and thankful hearts to our Maker."

Does this seems self-indulgent—to be celebrating so joyously when, beyond the walls of our assembly, people's lives are torn apart with suffering and injustice? Where do we get the strength and the simple dogged persistence to fight suffering and injustice? From many places, but surely among them is the gathered community refreshing its vision and its power in the joy—and the responsibility—of its common story, its common life.

So—prepared, informed, our tasks completed or put off until another day—let us enter the Sabbath.

Whatever is foreseen in joy
Must be lived out from day to
    day.
Vision held open in the dark
By our ten thousand days of
    work.
Harvest will fill the barn; for
    that
The hand must ache, the face
    must sweat.
And yet no leaf or grain is filled
By work of ours; the field is
    tilled
And left to grace. That we
    may reap,
Great work is done while we're
    asleep.
When we work well, a
    Sabbath mood
Rests on our day, and finds it
    good.

WENDELL BERRY

CHAPTER SEVEN

The Weekend: The Sabbath

Humanity troubles the earth for six days,
wrestling it, polluting it, trying to wrest a
livelihood from it. On the Sabbath or a
Sunday a truce is declared. . . . We try
to remind ourselves on that day of what a
universe at peace might be like.

GERALD SLOYAN

*A*hhh! The Sabbath has come. All week we have been filling our days, and often nights, with tasks—attending to work, dealing with leftover details, planning for the future.

But now! It is a time to let all the cares and tasks of the week—the drivenness of work, worries about the future—slip from our shoulders like a loosely held blanket, to observe and honor the Sabbath which, coming as it does from our Judeo-Christian heritage, has been described for our time as "a gift waiting to be unwrapped."

The Sabbath. A day to follow a different script. An opportunity, after six days of labor at trying to reshape the world to our liking, to "disconnect" from all of that and savor the *givenness* of life, its mystery and joy. Harvey Cox points out that the Hebrew word for God's resting used in the Fourth Commandment literally means "to catch one's breath." Our inner nod of recognition shows how much we need just such a day. There is a lot at stake here.

The observance of the Sabbath stands at the heart of Judaism. It has been considered the *sine qua non* of the Jews' survival, an affirmation of their faith and identity as a people. "More than the Jews have kept the Sabbath, the Sabbath has kept the Jews," goes an old saying.

What has been its nature? What does it look like today?

The concept of Sabbath, of *menuha*, had an early confirmation even before Moses received the Ten Commandments on Mount Sinai in the Hebrews' experience of manna, the life-giving bread which God provided for them in the desert after their escape from Egyptian slavery. They were to gather only enough for one day's need—except on the day preceding the Sabbath. On that day only, a double portion would be provided, so they could follow the commandment and observe the Sabbath as a day of rest.

> The Jewish tradition of Sabbath intimates a kind of wistful yearning for return to original creation. Sabbath is the way God intended life to be ordered, with a built-in rhythm of rest and refreshment. Yes, there is work to be done, but there is also, by God's grace, a respite from work, a day for rest, refreshment, renewal.
>
> KENNETH L. GIBBLE

The meaning of Sabbath has expanded since that time in the wilderness. By the time of the First Temple in the tenth century B.C.E., the Sabbath was associated with joy as well as rest. During the Second Temple period, in the first century C.E., practice of the Sabbath was the subject of intense and passionate debate. The sect known as the Sadducees was very ascetic, and stopped virtually all movement and all indoor illumination. The Pharisees, forerunners of the rabbis, permitted far more latitude, de-

claring Sabbath laws moot in instances of helping the sick
or saving a life.

Eventually, elaborate laws for what could and could
not be done were evolved by rabbinic tradition, and today

*Shabbat is not just law and
liturgy; it is also a shared way
of life, a set of activities that
become second nature, a round
of custom and prayer that the
youngest child or the oldest
invalid can enter, a piece of
time that opens space for
God.*

DOROTHY BASS

there is great variation on what
Jews consider appropriate Sabbath
observance. In Orthodox communities, Jews do not drive cars. In Israel
there have been efforts to block
roads on the Sabbath that lead
through Orthodox neighborhoods.
Variations are allowed. In some
neighborhoods an invisible bound-
ary has been agreed upon: Within
that space it is considered accept-
able to walk or wheel a baby carriage.

Traditionally, money is not handled. In observant Orthodox families, no serious business negotiations are
begun late in the afternoon on Friday, for fear they cannot be completed by sundown.

Orthodox Jews don't make any but emergency phone
calls on the Sabbath. Because of a Talmud restriction on
completing any construction on the Sabbath and because
a successful phone call completes an electrical circuit, a
rabbinical institute in Jerusalem has invented a Shabbat
phone, in which the dialing of a phone number interrupts
an already existing circuit. This is, and is recognized as,
an expedient and is used only for emergencies.

Sabbath is also a celebration of deliverance from op-
pression and a day for strengthening one's commitment
to justice for all: *All* are to rest, not just the rulers, the
privileged few. In the familiar commandment, "The seventh day is a Sabbath to the Lord your God; you shall not

do any work—you, your son or your daughter, your male or your female slave, your livestock, or the alien resident in your towns" (Exodus 20:10) it has been noted that "your wife" is conspicuously absent from this list, for what reason we can only conjecture. Maybe something has been lost in translation, or maybe this is an acknowledgment that *some* work is necessary to meet basic needs.

> To the eyes of outsiders, Jewish observance of the Sabbath can seem like a dreary set of restrictions, a set of laws that don't bear any good news. According to those who live each week shaped by Shabbat, however, it is a practice that powerfully alters their relationships to nature, work, God, and others.
>
> DOROTHY BASS

Orthodox Jews may see the Sabbath as acknowledging the freedom of God's will as revealed in the law, and Reform Jews may see the Sabbath as a symbol of universal and social morality and a hoped-for world of peace. But for all observant Jews, Sabbath is a day for singing, for rest, for good food, for giving and receiving blessings—a regular, intentional witness to what a perfect and blessed world might be like. Rabbinic guidelines even suggest Sabbath as a good time for married couples to have sex.

It is Friday evening at sundown. A family gathers around the table. The table is set for dinner—the best dishes, candles, a linen tablecloth instead of the customary place mats. The children have exchanged their play clothes for "best" clothes. The mother and father, too, are dressed as for a special occasion. Perhaps there are guests present. In what has been described as "the most evocative of all Jewish rituals" the mother strikes a match and lights the candles, reciting as she does so the ancient Jewish prayer for Sabbath eve: "Blessed art Thou, O Lord our God, King of the Universe, who hast sanctified us by Thy commandments, and commanded us to kindle the Sabbath lights." The Sabbath has begun. The candles lit, the family turns toward the door, singing a greeting to Shabbat, often personified as a bride, a radiant queen who brings delight and peace. The bread is there—the challah, the glistening braided loaf—and the cups of wine. Prayers of thanks are offered, and blessings for the food and wine. The father lays his hand on the head of each child in turn, and offers a blessing on behalf of that child. The family sits down to eat. It is a special time, and they will be more intentional in their conversation. Perhaps they will talk about some portion of the Torah.

Later they may attend services at the temple. There are services tomorrow morning, too. Perhaps they will go, perhaps not. The bulk of the day they will try to spend together, perhaps visiting family and friends.

At sundown on Saturday they gather again to observe the *Havdala*, the ceremony marking the close of the Sabbath. A special candle is lit—its doubled intertwined wick symbolizing the intertwining of worship and work. There are prayers, blessings, songs. A sweet-smelling spice—perhaps clove—is passed. Each member of the family inhales the fragrance. It is a symbol of taking the Sabbath with them through the coming week. The candle is extinguished. The room darkens. The Sabbath is over.

True, the children may giggle, self-conscious, as the father lays his hand in blessing on their heads. They may wish they had gone to the basketball game—and there will probably be times when they do that instead. But what is happening here is irreplaceable and profoundly affecting. They are declaring their freedom from a dominant culture that takes little time for respite, for honoring ancient traditions, for the cultivation of the soul. They are building for themselves and their children a plumb line of community, of belonging, a sense of the mystery of faith. They are paying honor to God, to whom honor is due, observing the rich traditions of their people, declaring themselves members of a community so that when they are alone or beset by life's inevitable terrors, there will be something there to sustain them, for they do not walk alone.

The Christian Sabbath, coming as it did from Jewish tradition, has, for the most part, shifted its location to Sunday. Notable exceptions are Seventh-Day Adventists and Seventh-Day Baptists. For a while the "modernist" church of Rome led the campaign to move the celebration of Sabbath from Saturday to Sunday, while the more traditionalist Eastern churches stayed with the Jewish practice of a Saturday Sabbath. But

Come, let us welcome the Sabbath in joy and peace! Like a bride, radiant and joyous, comes the Sabbath. It brings blessings to our hearts; workday thoughts and cares are set aside. The brightness of the Sabbath light shines forth to tell that the divine spirit of love abides within our home. In that light all our blessings are enriched, all our griefs and trials are softened.

FROM THE KIDDUSH RITUAL OF A RE-FORM HOME SERVICE FOR SABBATH EVE

in the mid-fourth century, the Roman Church won out, and the church officially abandoned the Saturday Sabbath observance in favor of Sunday. Centuries later, in the sixteenth century, Martin Luther, as part of his opposition to what he felt to be the legalism of the Catholic Church, declared any day as good as any other day. Worship should be daily, Luther decreed, but at least one day should be set aside for it. For most churches the custom of Sunday has prevailed. Some Christians have considered the hours of Sabbath to be sundown on Saturday to sundown on Sunday; others have observed from midnight to midnight, or from bedtime on Saturday until bedtime on Sunday. The Puritans, eager to reinforce their piety, extended the

Sabbath observance from 3 P.M. on Saturday until Monday morning.

But for a growing number of contemporary Christians, Sunday observance is an hour or two on Sunday morning, sandwiched in between the Sunday paper and a full afternoon of activities. Sometimes even an hour on Sunday morning is too much.

It was not always so! It is hard for us to realize how important and vital Sabbath observance was in early America and Europe. And, at least until the Puritans came along, it was a day to be enjoyed! Anglicans and Roman Catholics (as well as Eastern Orthodox) affirmed Sunday as a day for appreciating and enjoying God's gifts in all aspects of body, mind, and spirit.

Puritan influence, coming as it did out of a British culture where leisure time was often marked by brutal sports, drunkenness, gambling, fighting, bawdy theater, and general debauched idleness, added a different tone to Sunday observance. There had been, since before the time of Luther, prohibitions against "dancing, ribald singing, theater, and races in circuses," and the Puritans were very intentional in trying to bring human life more in accord with the divine nature as they understood it. In the American colonies they observed the strictest Sabbaths in Christian history, and these standards were enforced by law well into the nine-

A Song for the Sabbath:
Praise for the Lord's
Goodness

It is good to give thanks to the
Lord,
to sing praises to your name,
  O Most High;
to declare your steadfast love
  in the morning,
and your faithfulness by night,
to the music of the lute and the
  harp,
to the melody of the lyre.
For you, O Lord, have made
  me glad by your work;
at the works of your hands, I
  sing for joy.

PSALM 92:1-4

teenth century. Public worship was required, as well as private religious exercises; adherents were encouraged to perform acts of mercy, and to rest from bodily labors, with exceptions allowed where necessary—as with farmers who needed to tend to their crops and feed their animals. Recreation was generally limited to afternoons and, again, brutal sports were banned.

The extremes of the Puritan Sabbath were hard to take—its legalism, its denial of the playful and intuitive in worship and in life. Seeing how play could degenerate into debauchery, Puritans banned play on the Sabbath. Life must be viewed *seriously.* Besides denying the life-giving aspects of imagination and play, heavy seriousness could be exhausting, and Puritan Sabbaths were often grim and exhausting events.

But the American Puritan experiment with a "serious Sabbath" had its strengths. It was socially progressive, giving almost everyone a day of shared rest for spiritual awareness. It reinforced a shared Christian way of life located in a special day. Its appeal to scripture as the final authority gave people courage to withstand authoritarian pressures from church as well as state—something of a contradiction, considering the authoritarian nature of the Puritan state—as well as from overbearing employers.

But its dour and repressive influences fortunately could not last. Karl Barth chided his Puritan ancestors for making the Sabbath not only into a working day but into a bad working day of forced abstentions, pious exercises, and regulations blotting out the real obedience called for, which is to celebrate, rejoice, and be free, to the glory of God. He advocates instead a day of living without a program, free from any compulsion, a day filled with "a quality of lightness." The Second Vatican Council reemphasized the Lord's Day as a day of freedom from work and for the community to gather for the Eucharist—a return to the concept of the Lord's Day as "the original feast day," of joy as the appropriate mood for the day.

As inheritors of all of that weighty history and conflicting suggestions, how are we to celebrate—assuming we want to—the Christian Sabbath at the end of the twentieth century?

The scene shifts to another family. It's Sunday morning now, not Friday evening. Breakfast has been a little later than usual this morning, maybe a little more leisurely. But now the dishes are cleaned up and the family is getting ready for church—maybe for Sunday school, too.

Assembled, the family piles into the car, maybe taking their Bibles and study books, and sets off for church. Once arrived they will siphon off to their separate classes in a variety of subject matters—Bible study, studies of social issues looked at through the lens of Christianity, ways of praying, perhaps a session of personal sharing of what is going on in their lives. After Sunday school the family reassembles, goes together to the worship service, nodding to friends and acquaintances—and strangers—as they gather in the sanctuary, which can be anything from a small multipurpose room to an elaborate Gothic setting. For the next hour they will join in singing, prayers, attending to scripture and sermon, voiced concerns of the pastor and the congregation, thanksgivings for events that have occurred during the week, perhaps participation in the rite of Holy Communion or baptism. The choir will sing, there may be an offering of sacred dance. Perhaps some new members join the congregation.

Yes, the children may get fidgety. Sometimes early in

the service there is a special message for children, after which they may be dismissed to attend activities more attuned to their needs. If not, it helps to have a pad and crayons along, or a roll of Life Savers candy for discreet consumption. I recall with great affection sitting in the family pew beside my mother and holding her hand, turning the diamond ring on her finger until it caught the rays of sunlight coming in through the stained-glass window, and the various shared stories and innuendoes we absorbed over the years of attending church together as a family—such as the Sunday morning when the elderly woman who sat in the pew adjoining ours, upon hearing read from the pulpit the controversially liberal governor's thanksgiving proclamation with its concluding words, "God save the Commonwealth of Massachusetts," muttered with great feeling, "You can say that again!"

Religious enlightenment? No. But a rich well of living within that religious community so that even now—many years after I moved away from that town—when I return and pass that red sandstone building, which has, since its church days, served as travel agency, denominational headquarters, and who knows what else, my heart turns to it in recognition and gratitude. I was taken there as an infant, counted my birthday pennies into the birthday basket at Sunday school, was baptized and confirmed in that church, was married there. Of course it is my home. My special place of belonging is that pew on the right, under the window, about half way down the aisle, where I sometimes wondered when on earth the anthem would end (Why were they singing the same words over and over again—didn't they know we'd already heard them?), and when the minister would stop preaching. But again, something is being laid down here—a sense of a community of belonging, a range of adult figures to whom one is linked by virtue of doing something important together, a rare occasion for members of the family to be physically quiet and attentive together for a sustained period of time. A sense of the hush and mystery of worship, a groping toward God.

After church there may be a coffee hour, or maybe a meal, offered to anyone who comes. There are certainly friends to greet, new people to welcome, expressed concerns to be followed up by a word of personal support. In big-city churches a special effort is often made to welcome the stranger, make those who may be lonely or alone feel welcomed, cherished, at home.

My husband tells of, years ago, going alone on a Sunday morning to a big-city church known for its welcome to visitors. Before the service he was approached by a parishioner who said he'd spotted him as a stranger and asked whether he'd like to join a group of young adults going to lunch together. Yes, he would. After the meal together at a Chinese restaurant the group—part visitors, part a core of parish members—walked through the park, visited a museum, returned to the church for a small-group gathering, then for a small informal service, and then for coffee hour. He remembers that it was at least 10 P.M. when he returned to the place he was staying. This particular church has a reputation for offering extended hospitality to visitors, but it is not unusual, particularly in large cities where there may be a lot of lonely people, for churches to make of Sunday a community day in which to gather and celebrate what is perhaps the most basic community of our lives, and so find meaning and pattern for all the relationships of the week.

My husband and I met in the basement of such a church on a Sunday evening, in what would now be called a singles' group, and it became the social and spiritual matrix for much of our life together for the next two years. As our relationship deepened and grew, the group became a kind of background community, a safe and congenial environment in which we could play out some of the stages of our growing interest in and commitment to each other. The group's heterogeneity was part of its charm.

One member regularly carried a pet hamster in his pocket and fished it out during the social hour for everyone to enjoy. My only (so far) Rosicrucian friend was a member of that group, as was a Unitarian who was totally unfamiliar with Christian scripture and was therefore an astonished perceiver of the radical nature of the Christian gospel when he began to read it for himself. For many of us—students, young working people—the group was our home away from home. When my husband and I decided to marry, these friends were among the first to know and rejoice with us, and several of them traveled many miles in winter weather to be with us at our wedding.

I have digressed from our representative family experiencing a Christian Sabbath. And yet I have not. Experiences such as these—the extended and generous welcome of the stranger, the identification in strange and sometimes puzzling ways with a group who finds their community home in church and relishes and celebrates that together—are what the Sabbath is all about and are some of the many faces the Sabbath wears in its exchanges with the world.

What about the rest of this family's Sabbath? Probably

they go home or to a restaurant for Sunday dinner—usually the main meal of the day, a time for relaxed conversation, maybe with reference to the morning service, the news of friends, announced activities to contemplate.

Many families have their own rituals about Sunday dinner. I remember the fragrance of the roast in the oven as we came into the house after church. As quickly as we could, we would assemble the meal. Often there would be visitors—usually issued an impromptu invitation by my mother if she saw someone who looked a bit at loose ends. Sometimes the minister and his wife would join us. My aunt and uncle and grandmother were often guests at our table. On one occasion my mother invited a friend, a middle-aged single woman, a pillar of the church, whom we had recently learned had an alcohol problem. If anything was said about it I didn't hear it, and I doubt that there was. My mother (and father—though it was usually my mother who leaned toward these impromptu invitations) wanted her to know that they loved and valued her and that in no way was there to be any stigma against her at this house.

A feature of our Sunday dinner for a number of years was the ritual, when the meal was done, of my brother's bringing a certain section of the Sunday paper to the table and asking the assembled family "The Riddles and Posers." My impression is that neither of these quizzes was sufficiently taxing that among us someone could not come up with a plausible answer. On the occasions when we missed, my brother took some satisfaction in being the

Sunday is also a day to notice the world, to see that the world is there . . . Sunday is a day to walk, not to ride. It is a day to look, much better than looking, it is a day to see.

GERALD SLOYAN

maestro—he with the riddles and posers, and the answers, to dispense.

After dinner, the freedom of the afternoon opened up. Maybe a nap for some, a leisurely reading of the Sunday paper, or a book for which there seemed to have been no time during the week. A generation or so ago, a favorite Sunday afternoon pastime was a family drive in the country. The crunch and fragrance of a cold McIntosh apple will always connote to me those Sunday-afternoon drives in the hills of western Massachusetts, where we would stop at the apple farm and, after extended contemplation of the varieties of apples, would purchase a basket or two.

Once a year we would organize a blueberry-picking expedition for Sunday. And another Sunday afternoon in the spring—when my father sensed it was time for the arbutus to be out—we would take paper bags and drive the several miles to the wooded area where arbutus trailed over the damp ground in spring, and, stooping low, darting from site to site as one of us would find a particularly rich patch of the tiny pink and white flowers, fill our bags—and subsequently our house—with the wafting fragrance of arbutus. On summer Sunday afternoons we would often take our bathing suits and a picnic supper to a family club along the river, returning home as dusk deepened into darkness and the younger children had fallen asleep and had to be wakened to stagger into the house and to bed. Or sometimes we'd drive the hour or so to share the afternoon with my father's cousin and his family. They lived along the river in a house set against a hillside, down which a waterfall cascaded and where, at the top of the hill and out of sight, was a family cemetery where generations of my father's New England forebears were buried.

As I got older, there were things I did on my own or with friends—go ice skating, or bike riding, or attending a youth group meeting at the church. Or things I would do in solitude. I have particular recall of, on several Sunday afternoons, getting out my watercolor paint set and, sitting at the dining room table, tracing forms and figures in watery pastel shades. Television was in the dim future then, and the mood in the house was one of quiet expectation. I cherish the memory of those times of being thrown on my own—a recourse against boredom or loneliness.

Our experience of Sunday often concluded with a hymn sing around the piano in the living room—a custom echoed in a similar gathering of extended families at a New Hampshire camp where we spent a week or two each summer and the normally reserved New England Congregationalists would sing, from tattered gospel songbooks, oldtime camp-meeting songs about wayward travelers struggling for deliverance from sin. There was one summer when, as sophisticated nonconforming adolescents, some of us boycotted the hymn sing. We returned soon enough, singing our way through with exchanged glances of conspiratorial nonbelief. But we knew we were missing too much to stay away for long.

Our Sunday-evening family hymn sings around the piano at home concluded, for at least a year or two, with my small brother's request to sing the song with which his Sunday-school hour concluded: "Our Sunday School is over, and we are going home. Good-bye, good-bye, be always kind and true." We sang it with straight faces, suppressed merriment, and full hearts.

Though it is beyond the scope of this book to give anything like a full treatment of Islamic practice, one cannot write of Sabbath as nourishing a relationship with God without acknowledging the growing number of Muslims in America. There are presently more than 5 million Muslims—a population almost equal in size to the Jewish population.

Since there are no parishes, Muslims attend whatever mosque they choose. Mosques, or *masjids,* range in size from little storefront *masjids* to major Islamic centers with schools, publications, huge Friday worship atttendance and salaried staffs. Friday being the Muslim day for congregational prayer, at mid-day on Friday the congregation gathers. Furnishings in the mosque are simple—no chairs or benches, but a series of carpets or mats, as people kneel or stand throughout the service. Facing toward Mecca, the worshippers declare their intention to pray. A series of postures—bending the body, standing upright, kneeling, touching the ground with their heads, then resting quietly on their knees, sitting on their feet—are part of the worship experience. At each position certain words are spoken. "The Opener," the first sura of the Quran, the holy book of Islam revealed to the prophet Mohammed, is always recited:

> *In the name of God, the Merciful, the Compassionate.*
> *Praise be to God, the Lord of the Worlds,*
> *The Merciful, the Compassionate,*
> *Master of the Day of Judgment.*
> *You we worship; you we ask for help.*
> *Guide us in the straight path,*
> *The path of those whom you have blessed,*

Not the path of those who have incurred your wrath,
Nor of those who have gone astray.

There will be other prayers, recitations from the Quran, followed by silent recitations of personal prayer, greetings, and salutations of peace to the prophet and to each other. A sermon is often given. While children do not customarily attend services in the mosque they do participate in family rituals at home. By third grade they have probably memorized sections of the Quran. The rhythms of Muslim life—the daily periods of prayer, training in the Quran, observance of special seasonal events such as patterns of fasting during the month of Ramadan—surround Muslim children with a sense of history and heritage, of the larger community of belief and practice to which they belong.

While my own preference and experience is toward honoring the Sabbath in a religious context, there are many people for whom these settings are not congenial. For them, while they do not have the resonance of a historical religious community in which to find a home, there are many ways in which they appropriate some of the qualities of Sabbath to make their lives richer, more reflective, more congruent with what seems to be a necessary rhythm of work and rest.

Some of the ways to appropriate Sabbath rest we will look at more fully in the next chapter, but for now let's consider another family. Again, it's Sunday morning. The parents have slept in—for as long as the children can be mollified by Sunday-morning cartoons. Perhaps a special breakfast together. They have planned a Sunday at the beach. They gather their swimming things—"Don't forget the sunblock!"—and their hamper of food: favorite sandwiches, chunks of cold melon, potato chips, a favorite salad, and some of mother's special brownies. They'll leave room for a couple of boxes of fried clams, which they'll get from the vendors at the beach. Some books to read, and a beach umbrella to crawl under when the sun is at its zenith. They may get too hot, have to contend with sand flies, keep cautioning one another about sunburn. But they'll have a wonderful time, and when they get home—hot, tired, their towels full of beach sand— they'll sit around in the cool of their house finishing up the lemonade and brownies and figuring out when they can do it again. By Monday the sting of the sunburn will have faded, and they'll be ready to enter a new week of work, as though they had come from a different world.

> No one ought to be so leisured as to take no thought in that leisure for the interest of his neighbor, nor so active as to feel no need for the contemplation of God. . . . It is love of truth that looks for sanctified leisure, while it is the compulsion of love that undertakes righteous engagement in affairs.
>
> AUGUSTINE

Today's young families have a wider range of options for the use of Sabbath time than families did a generation or so ago. Television presents new opportunities, and new dangers. A trip to a museum with a stop for ice cream may supplant a walk in the woods. Little League practice may require special configuring of the afternoon. Still, the day can have its own life, its attendant memories of "what we do together." As children grow to adulthood and make their own decisions, the legacy of such memories will weight the scale in favor of the Sabbath as a special day for family refreshment and common enterprise.

And, of course, not everyone travels in clans. Sometimes a day of solitary Sabbath calms the mind and heart, resets the priorities, enables one to enter a new workweek with a sense of refreshment and peace. A close friend, used to being with people all during the week, tells how one of the choicest experiences of his life was taking an overnight hike on the Appalachian Trail, alone. Sometimes, indeed, we feel most in communion with others when we are alone. In Russian there is a word for solitude that means "being with everyone."

But alone or in groups, in church, or temple, or mosque, or on a strip of sand along the beach, let's look at some of the ways we can make our Sabbath a day full of rest and gladness.

~⌀

CHAPTER EIGHT

Habits for Successful Sabbaths: Balancing the Day

*W*hether or not we choose to attend a religious service as part of our Sabbath, we can make this day a time that has a different quality from the rest of our week, a day that is truly refreshing.

A day of Sabbath rest doesn't need to be a passive day, a day when we sit around and do nothing—though if that is what brings us true refreshment of soul, that's one legitimate use of the day.

We'll need, at least to some extent, to decide whether we want a carefully put together Sabbath, or a take-it-as-it-comes day? Quiet or noisy, restful or action-packed? Do we want to tiptoe through the Sabbath, or romp through it?

Gerald Sloyan, himself a Catholic priest, has this prescription: "I have in mind a healthy measure of doing our own thing, whether it be playing the piano badly or reading the wedding notices at length or the 'Irish sports column,' the obituaries, or watching Lawrence Spivak or tennis matches or our national autumn madness on August 3 in Canton, Ohio, at ninety-eight degrees. It does not have to be morally uplifting. There is a sense in which, just because it is not, it will be. I mean by that that if you try to make it morally uplifting it will not refresh you. It has to be recreative. That means that it will often enough be done in the company of others and have no special purpose beyond being in their company."

Hopefully, we recognize the mood, though we might couch it in different terms. It is a mood of freedom, a mood of celebration, a mood that separates us from the workaday world of striving and getting.

And to what end? The day presents us with a whole new range of possible goals. Here are a few:

To balance the activism of our lives with the gift of quiet repose where we release ourselves for this period of time from the "oughts" and the "shoulds" of our usual busy life.

To enhance our family life by a period of time when we strengthen our ties to one another in a time of celebration and closeness.

To free up some time to perform some act of mercy—a visit to a sick person, some talk on the phone with a friend who needs us.

To get off the productive achievement ladder for one day at least, and rest in just being alive.

I don't spend all day Sunday at home—we go to church and often out to eat or to a movie or play or concert—but what I do with Sunday's home hours is most telling. Can I be home without being hell-bent on making check marks on a to-do list? It is a challenge. To help out I have another list, one of Sunday pastimes, to refer to: board games, potluck dinners, picnics, a long yoga set, reading for pleasure or inspiration, taking advantage of long-distance rates, practicing calligraphy, brushing the cats, playing with the dog, giving myself a facial, and seeing people who make me happy.

VICTORIA MORAN

To engage in some off-time vocation—painting, sailing, reading, for which the rest of the week allows little time.

Whatever focus—or lack of it—we choose, we will not glean from this day the gifts it offers if we do not make a part of this day what was integral to it from its first biblical injunction, the achievement of true rest.

Achievement? Not another duty! you think. Isn't rest exactly the opposite of achievement? Isn't rest the dropping of tasks—and now you're telling me it's something else to work for?

Of course. But in our harried, fragmented world, rest has to be a conscious decision and a decision implemented by certain changes of mind-set and planning, or we will bring to our periods of supposed rest the same preoccupations and concerns that permeate much of our weekday activity. (Am I resting now? What about that project I could be finishing so that I could really rest? Isn't this a little artificial? Couldn't I just think restful thoughts while getting some work done?)

Probably all of us warm to the idea of Sabbath rest—whether in church or temple or backyard swing—or a combination of many elements. The question is, how to pull it off?

Here are some suggestions that may work for you. Much is made of the habits of highly successful people. These are some habits for successful Sabbath observance.

Habit is a key word here. Of course there are many

> The meaning of the Sabbath is to celebrate time rather than space. Six days a week we live under the tyranny of things of space; on the Sabbath we try to become attuned to *holiness in time*. It is a day on which we are called upon to share in what is eternal in time, to turn from the results of creation to the mystery of creation; from the world of creation to the creation of the world.
>
> ABRAHAM JOSHUA HESCHEL

Sabbath occasions that come spontaneously into our lives, and other times when we'll have to desert our Sabbath pattern. If, however, we are to make of Sabbath a truly important component of life, we have to do it regularly, make it a rule of life. We'll have to use our Sabbath pattern consistently enough so that when those occasions come during which we have to depart from it, we'll sense we're really missing something, we'll have laid down enough deposit of Sabbath keeping that there's a layer of custom and expectation thick enough to stumble over when we choose to forgo it. Think how much energy and time you'd lose if you had to decide every day whether or not to brush your teeth! So, some habits for Sabbath keeping.

The habit of adopting a Sabbath mind-set. The habit of relinquishing weekday concerns. We'll probably have to continue to work at this throughout the Sabbath—so hard is it for most of us to set our worries and preoccupations aside—but if we can, before we enter the Sabbath it would be well to consciously dismiss for the next twenty-four hours our worries about our work, our health, our children, the state of our nation and our world. The admonition to Jews is that in observing the Sabbath, they lay aside even their grief. This day is a fresh creation, seen as through the words of Julian of Norwich: "All shall be well, and all shall be well, and all manner of thing will be well." Because "if this is the Sabbath, it must be Jerusalem."

The habit of paying attention—sometimes called Being Present Where You Are. Whatever use we make of Sabbath time—attendance at church or temple or mosque, a trip to the lake, a solitary swing in the hammock in the backyard— the ability to attend to the moment is probably a *sine qua non.* Herbert Benson's *Relaxation Response,* with its emphasis on deep breathing, helps focus attention on the moment.

Joan Baez speaks of prayer as "paying attention." Thich Nhat Hanh, in *The Miracle of Mindfulness,* writes of washing a teapot with reverence. Writer and teacher Sven Birkerts in a symposium on "The Reader in the Electronic Age" says, in decrying how diffuse much of our attention has become, "It is better, more rewarding, to look at a grasshopper on a windowsill with full attention than to stand half distractedly before a Klee or a Botticelli."

> The Sabbath is not a running away from problems, but the opportunity to receive grace to face them.
>
> MARVA DAWN

The habit of letting go. This has many faces, and each of us will discover what our own particular compulsions are. Are we compelled to keep our noses to the grindstone because if we eased up on our responsibilities the world would crumble? A story is told of a man called George Singer, civic leader, involved in all sorts of good works, who felt himself about to get sick and, fuming against the prospect of lost time, fell asleep and dreamed he saw the Lord God Almighty pacing the floor of heaven, wringing his hands and saying, "What shall I do? What shall I do? George Singer is about to get sick." The world will do fine if we relax our hold on it for twenty-four hours.

The habit of curbing ambition (at least for today). Well to remember on any day of the week, but especially on the Sabbath, is a tale of a rich industrialist from the North who was horrified to find a southern fisherman lying leisurely beside his boat. "Why aren't you fishing?" asked the industrialist.

"Because I have caught enough fish for the day," said the fisherman.

"Why don't you catch some more?"

"What would I do with it?"

"You could earn more money," said the industrialist. "With that you could fix a motor to your boat, go into deeper waters and catch more fish. Then you could make enough money to buy nylon nets. These would bring you more fish and more money. Soon you would have enough money to own two boats—maybe even a fleet of boats. Then you would be a rich man like me."

"What would I do then?"

"Then you could really enjoy life."

Said the fisherman, "What do you think I am doing right now?"

Habits such as these—and you can add your own—will enhance the rest of our lives as well.

> We must consciously slow down the pace on Sunday. Otherwise we shall have a great outlet of energy in liturgical activity or meal preparation or athletic contests on that day, alternating with exhaustion. It will be a day of mad highs and lows: new ways to grow tired, which is the diametric opposite of rest.
>
> GERALD SLOYAN

Of course we will not always be able to keep these Sabbath habits alive. But maybe we will experience in the effort to try them out enough refreshment to try again. When we fail there is no need to berate ourselves—the last thing we need is something else to feel guilty about!

So, with our habits in place and our spirits geared for freedom, what shall we do? Each of us will find our own balance among the choices that commend themselves to us.

What is labor for some may be Sabbath rest for others. On our way to church we drive past a Laundromat. It is always busy, even on Sunday. This isn't my way to honor the Sabbath, but I have friends who have experienced the Laundromat as a pleasant getaway—a place to read, to chat with neighbors, to get away from the furor of a busy household.

In that same vein, a "Sunday painter" finds restoration and new life with an easel and canvas and brushes, while an artist who paints for a living would do well to close the door of the studio as a way of entering the Sabbath. A professional cook might choose to stay out of any kitchen, while for a bookkeeper or lawyer, cooking could be a true feast for the soul as well as the body.

"What do you like to do on Sunday afternoon?" I ask a friend. It takes her less than a minute to decide. "I like to have dinner with friends, then stretch out on the sofa with the Sunday paper and the cats, until we all fall asleep."

All of us have a rich lode of memory from which to draw in our search for the qualities of peace, refreshment, and delight, which also helps us to know what we are looking for in our search for a Sabbath mind-set, a Sabbath expectation, a Sabbath rest. What are your own favorite associations with Sunday? I have already mentioned some: a blueberry picking day, some solitary painting while the rest of the family naps, reading some things I don't have time to get to during the week. Others come to mind—a Sunday afternoon when my husband and I and our four children went to a neighborhood field to fly kites—an experience imprinted on our minds by the memory of our four-year-old son saying, while observing his father running along the field in repeated unsuccessful attempts to get the kite airborne, "Oh, this is so embarrassing."

The habit of spending time with family. "Family time" seems a favorite association for many. Rides in the country—if you can find easy country roads anymore. A family walk in the woods. In wry contradiction to such movements toward togetherness, I recall the long-ago words of the comedian George Gobel, who suggested on his television show, "And remember folks—if you want a nice Sunday afternoon ride in the country, leave the wife and kiddies at home." Some people do prefer solitude, at least for part of the day.

What other family associations? We are learning that foods have emotional as well as nutritional value. Are there favorite foods that connote security or Sabbath joy to you? Can you incorporate them as part of your Sabbath? I have only to taste homemade banana ice cream and I am back there sitting at my family's Sunday dinner table, with my brother starting off with those Riddles and Posers.

The habit of enjoying a change of scene. Sacred places. Sacred because they have become so. A grove of trees beside a brook where watercress grows—another site of a Sunday-afternoon family walk. A turnstile in a field divided by fences—a surprising discovery—"Look, children. This is what a turnstile looks like." Up and over, down the other side. The childhood stories with turnstiles now at last made real many years later—a Sunday-afternoon outing. A small mountain lake in New Hampshire where I spent vacation Sundays with my parents. Even to think of it evokes the true rest of Sabbath. "The Sabbath of location." My own experience on a Sunday afternoon of leaving the turmoil of a summer job working (almost around the clock) with young children, and driving with several other counselors through the green slopes of the Catskill Mountains to lie on the grass outside the music shed at Tanglewood and listen to the music waft out over us. When, many years later, I returned to Tanglewood to hear my son sing under that same shed, the memory of my visit and of all the ensuing years went with me and hovered in the green and blue afternoon, lifting my parental pride even higher into the sky above the Berkshires.

The habit of setting the stage. In setting the stage for the experience of Sabbath, it may be helpful to close your eyes and enter a reverie in which you invite the luminous experiences of your life to come forward and remind you of what they were. The process of reflection might be likened to our family's experience of visiting Ruby Falls in the caves of Tennessee. At the climactic moment of the tour the lights were turned out; in that total darkness a searchlight fell on the falls. One has to be still—and maybe removed from the distraction of all the sights around one—to see the magic.

Some old men came to see Abba Poemen, and said to him: Tell us, when we see brothers dozing during the sacred office, should we pinch them so they will stay awake? The old man said to them: Actually, if I saw a brother sleeping, I would put his head on my knees and let him rest.

DESERT WISDOM

From the wealth of our own recovered images and feelings, and from the words of friendly guides, perhaps we can each set our own personal code for Sabbath observance.

What might that be?

I have made references earlier to some of these choices regarding what to do. Stay away from Laundromats—unless that's a place of restoration for you. Another—reschedule a lot of utilitarian labor that could be done another day. A woman tells of her habit at one time of making a pot of stew on Sunday afternoon to see her through heavy exam periods in her teaching. But then she decided that no, its encroachment on the Sabbath was not worth the benefit of having the stew already prepared, and she found she could work that domestic task in during the week and regain the freedom of her Sabbath. One is reminded of the misguided Israelites who went out to gather manna on the day of rest and found none, but did find that the double portion they had been instructed to gather on the day preceding the Sabbath kept over just fine for the Sabbath meal (Exodus 16:21–30).

A man tells how, in honor of creation, he has given up on the Sabbath all but the most urgent uses of his car. This is, of course, in line with the orthodox position in Judaism of going only where you can walk.

A writer tells of her early move toward Sabbath keeping being the decision not to turn on her word processor. "That way at least I wasn't working for money, even if I did sneak in a load of laundry. This evolved over time into a genuine day of rest, a day that has enriched my relationships, increased my creativity, and substantially improved my health. I think I used to get colds because I couldn't get off the overachievement treadmill any other way. I don't catch cold as readily anymore. And I love Sunday now; it's the one day I don't have to produce. I can just experience."

Often Sabbath is the occasion for seeing people we care about but whom we have difficulty seeing during the week. The classic pattern of dating on weekends is an example of this—as I remember so well from the time I was dating my husband, and college life kept him busy until noon on Saturday. Saturday afternoons and evenings, and again on Sunday, we spent together.

The habit of creating rituals for families. Now that the

old prohibitions against movies, dancing, loud noise, card playing—you name it—no longer apply, are there ways families can enhance their Sabbath experience?

It is important that Sabbath be different from the rest of the week's activities. My husband's father grew up in a family where the game cupboard was full and often visited. But there were Sunday games and weekday games and the father in the family, who made the decree, said he didn't care which were which, but they should be different. Some families make Sabbath the time to visit extended family members or friends who may be lonely or in need of special attention. Some families have a pattern of keeping the TV turned off. Others may find programs they like to watch together and make a habit of doing that.

Some families—Christian as well as Jewish—who may or may not attend a service at temple or church—make a practice of having family worship services at home as a way of marking their Sabbath observance. This may take place on Friday evening, to welcome the Sabbath, or as a way of closing out the Sabbath on Sunday evening.

Chances are one member of the family (usually a parent) will find

Soup Kitchen Sabbath

All week I spend hours sitting.
Thinking a path through agendas.
Cooking up messages of fast-
flavored words.
Reading agendas, interpreting
notes.
Tied to a desk. Excited by
thoughts.
Or following the herd from
home to work, work to
home.
This daily labor is good. It is
worth my time, worth my
life . . .

Then the Sabbath sets a new pace.
We peel a pile of carrots. And
slice several pounds of bread.
Trays on a table call for
stacking 200 knives, 200
forks, 200 spoons.

The people themselves are all hungry, but few come just for food.
Some are homeless, some are
seniors, some are children.

We need to know all the shelters, ask the children how school is going, show the parents the clothing that has come, introduce some people to AA, and discover who's missing this week, and why.

This Sabbath service is good. It is worth our time, worth our lives.

DEE WORD HORN

the idea appealing; bringing the rest of the family in on the planning is important. Do we want to do this? Why? And then how? It is probably well to start slowly—maybe once a month. Some religious groups have prescribed orders of service for such a gathering. If not, such a service might include singing, a scripture reading, prayers of gratitude and blessing for each family member, any particular concerns of each one, prayers for clarity in seeing our role in the world. Are there special people and causes that need our help? What can we do to be helpful? The service might close with the family joining hands and singing a favorite song. Then maybe some popcorn and milk, or some other snack.

Ernest Boyer, Jr., in *A Way in the World: Family Life as Spiritual Discipline*, has these suggestions for a Sabbath family worship:

1. Keep it short and simple.

2. Find a way for as many as possible to take part.

3. Do not rely only on words; find simple symbolic gestures to represent the important parts of family life.

4. Come to recognize the power of repetition.

5. Invite others to join you.

6. Have fun.

It won't be an easy venture, making a go of family worship—particularly as children grow into adolescence and want to do what their peers are doing—but for some families it is definitely worth a try. Probably for young children a special family occasion on a day when peers are doing something else is no big deal. Doing something pleasant together as a family is a value beyond most other values. At any age the capacity to be different is a precious gift, though to do that as "Operation Dullsville" is not. Problems are apt to arise as the children grow to adolescence and the world of ball games, movies with friends, television that "everyone" is watching may call to them with increasing urgency. A mild protest as a sign of independence is one thing; an adamant spurning of the occasion may outweigh the values it offers. But even an abandoned custom will leave its residue of remembered closeness, a sense of "what we were about" as something important.

> The one thing the attempt [at family worship] cannot survive is becoming Operation Dullsville. If the kids hate it—and being at all different is something they are going to resist from the start—it's a gone goose. Whatever is tried has to have numerous short-term, pleasurable rewards . . . A Sunday on a slower pace has above all to show signs of life.
>
> GERALD SLOYAN

"How is this day different from any other day?" the youngest child present asks at the Jewish Seder service. Some months ago I was at a reception at a summer inn, chatting with a woman I'd never met before. In the course of the conversation the subject turned to vocation and, learning that I am a writer, she asked me what I was working on now. When I told her it was a book about Sabbath, her interest heightened. "We recently retired," she told me. "A few weeks ago I realized all our days were running together, all the same. So we decided to make Sab-

Sunday morning

After a special breakfast, our house falls into *silence* for an hour. Each family member goes to his/her room or to some other place alone. It is the only waking hour in the week when the house is silent: you can feel the stillness opening and inviting a reflective mind sensitive to the spirit among us. . . . As my wife has told me, "It is hard to be good without something to be good with." She once read our children an English novel that made reference to a special box of aids for a family of children during Sunday quiet time. That led us, when the children were young, to develop a "sabbath box" for each of them, brought out only on Sundays, containing things like water colors, sketch pads, and new books. The children often spontaneously create things they enjoy making and give them to us or to each other, or otherwise share their experiences at the end of quiet time.

TILDEN EDWARDS

bath a special day. We go to temple. Then we spend the rest of the day visiting family and friends, maybe getting some extra rest."

"Wonderful!" I said. "Do you mind if I quote you in my book?"

"Not at all. And it's really made a difference in our lives."

As obvious from some of the activities described, experiences evoking Sabbath rest don't have to be "religious." "Spiritual" is a different matter. And they obviously don't have to take place on Sunday, or Saturday, or Friday.

In some cases they can't. For clergy, of course the Sabbath may be the busiest workday of all. In the years when my husband was a pastor, we tried at least to reserve Friday evening as a time for the family to be together. During his earliest years when we had four preschool children (and before the days when children customarily went to preschool at a very young age) we really needed a Sabbath for ourselves. We were fortunate in being able to hire a fine woman to care for our children, and in nice weather, on one day a week, we would pack a lunch, get in the car, and take a long drive out into the country—the less-populated the better—usually to some previously unvisited terrain; we would stop at midday at some roadside woods or picnic area and savor the scenery and the food and the quiet and the pleasure of each other's company. Perhaps we'd read aloud from a book we'd brought along. We would come back refreshed, ready to pick up again with the clamor of our family and parish duties—and be planning where we would go the following week on our day away.

There are many other vocations that require work on the Sabbath—nursing jobs, restaurant workers, and, increasingly, department store workers. Jewish merchants in many nations have long had to accommodate to a culture in which their Sabbath is among the busiest shopping days of the week. My son, an airline pilot, often flies weekends and is on those times unable to join his wife and children at church and other Sabbath-day activities.

What other experiences of Sabbath—on whatever day of the week? Another son takes his two small daughters, one at a time because the difference in their ages makes their stamina unequal, on a hike up a particular favorite mountain. I expect it is a Sabbath of sorts for him, and for them, and that they will look back on these hikes as among the treasures of their childhood.

Others—random events that betoken Sabbath? A sunny morning on an isolated mountaintop when, yearning for some sign of God's presence, I saw two birds join in a song in a nearby tree and felt my prayer had been answered. Books? Were there books that seemed so right for you at the time you could almost believe you were *meant* to read them? I recall as a young woman, just out of college and in my first job, coming upon Thoreau's *Walden*.

My perceptions of the life immediately around me were so sharpened that I got up an hour earlier than usual each day and took the book into the wooded glen near my apartment to read it in the freshness of the spring morning. Coming home to fix breakfast, the pouring of cereal and milk into a bowl seemed somehow a sacred oblation, the slicing of a banana an act of worship. I finished reading the book and soon thereafter my life returned to its more mundane tenor, but I remember those days as gifts of clearness and gratitude.

Much earlier—maybe in sixth or seventh grade—I took from my parents' bookshelf a slim volume, bound in purple with gold tooling and printed on fine parchment-like paper and read through Henry Van Dyke's long poem "The Toiling of Felix." For the first time I felt almost a physical charge of excitement and recognition that words could fall on the page *exactly right* and that maybe some day I might have a part in that alchemy. That book has a place of honor on my bookshelf now. Rilke's *Letters to a Young Poet*. Frederick Buechner's *Alphabet of Grace*. Even to say these titles to myself evokes an expansion of the heart.

There are many other ways to remind ourselves of the possibilities within Sabbath rest for what I would call Sabbath illumination—a sense of peace, beauty, a trust that one is in the right place. A sense of all the tributaries of one's life flowing in the same direction. Ashley Montague describes the mood of playgoers leaving the theater after a moving drama and speculates that this sense of heightened mutual appreciation that is almost sacred is something humankind can aspire to on a broader scale. This is part of what people who attend services of worship are searching for. But, again, these searchings and findings don't have to be in religious terms. My husband recalls a trip as a boy with his father when they took the overnight train from Pittsburgh to the Chicago World's Fair. He can tell you, almost moment by moment, the events as they unfolded that day, until he and his dad boarded the overnight train again for the trip home. It became part of the genesis of his lifelong love of trains, and people might speak of the Kingdom of God on earth with scarcely more reverence and delight than he tells of that day with his father.

Again, experiences of Sabbath don't have to be religious and they don't have to occur on your Sabbath day. Sometimes they just have to be recognized—as extra gifts, enriching the whole concept of Sabbath in our lives.

So, assume you are committed to making a life change, to make the Sabbath in some form a pattern of your life. In addition to the stories, the principles, and guidelines, here are a few warnings, a few bewares.

Beware of too-casual shifts in your plan to observe Sabbath. One week missed is okay—we all occasionally have things that interfere with our best resolves. But you need to develop the *habit* of Sabbath observance, so that there is a sort of *givenness* to the expectation of the day. The painter Monet is said to have returned each day to the scene of his haystacks and waited, brushes in hand, until the same light illumined the haystacks again. A constancy of habit and expectation.

Beware of easy distractions, including duties you feel called to perform. There will always be someone who needs something from you. There will always be tasks raising their heads and saying, in effect, "Just this once. You'll feel much freer if you attend to me first." It's a ploy. Don't believe it.

Beware of being too hard on yourself. The temptation to give it all up if it seems somehow difficult (even artificial) can easily dissolve into abandoning the whole resolve. As they say about bike riders who fall off—get up and start again, right away.

Beware of expecting too much too soon. You will have to trim and expand your plan for observing Sabbath. It may also take some time before Sabbath observance seems "natural," so that you're not spending half of your day thinking, "Is this wise? Think of all I could be accomplishing," etc. Remember, freedom from worry is one of the conditions of good Sabbath. Try it—you'll like it!

Beware of taking on too much—either at home, or place of worship—or agreeing to too-ambitious plans for social events. The rest of the day can easily be lost in exhausting overdoses of activity.

Beware of letting the day slip into heaviness. Play, and fun, are part of the healing and freeing qualities of true Sabbath. There used to be (maybe still is) a warning acronym among religious educators, YTYTDS, which stands for "You Take Yourself Too Damn Seriously." Lighten up! There is joy in the garden.

CHAPTER NINE

⟶

The Care and Feeding of Sabbath: Seasonal Milestones

$\mathcal{W}$e know how easily our Sabbath focus—our sense of peaceful rest in the midst of busyness—slips away. We yearn for more of the peace and perspective, the realization of what is truly important, that moments—or hours—of true Sabbath rest can bring us.

Inevitably, we do experience moments of clarity, of reevaluating our lives. Sometimes these occur at times of tragedy or crisis—a death in the family, the ambiguities of retirement. Some come at moments of special gladness, crises of a different sort—the birth of a baby, reprieve from the threat of serious illness. All of these experiences are "showstoppers" for any of us, and in the wake of such experiences perhaps we resolve not to let the rush of daily concerns cloud our perceptions again.

But we need more than good intentions, and while our weekly Sabbath observance is the food and drink of our spiritual life, we may need some "jump starts" from time to time to refresh our vision and recharge our batteries. Over the years faiths and cultures have developed seasonal patterns that help us do just that—keep our Sabbath observances fresh and generative.

There are seasons of life that we mark with special consideration. Celebrations of birth such as the Christian baptism and the Jewish *bris* welcome a new member into the community. A Muslim woman tells of observing a grandmother praying for a new baby and then blowing gently all over the infant's body—the breath of life transmitted from one generation to another. Occasions such as First Communion, Confirmation, Bar and Bat Mitzvahs, are religious observances to mark the onset of a new stage of physical and spiritual life. In marriage ceremonies couples share before the community their commitment to each other. Services for the blessing of a home acknowledge the significance of taking up our daily life in a different place. Rituals of mourning help us to say good-bye to our loved ones. Other occasions—a child's first day of school, the onset of puberty, the acquisition of a driver's license, graduation, the beginning of a new job, an academic sabbatical (for those fortunate enough to receive one!), a retirement party—also mark our passage through life, help ground us in the joys and sorrows of what it means to be human and, as such, give a kind of frame within which our Sabbath experiences find a home.

There are seasons and special days that recur each year and offer our spirits opportunity for renewal.

Summer is a time when children are not usually in school—a time for most of us, unless we work in a resort area, to relax our pace and perhaps take a vacation. It begins Memorial Day weekend, is increasingly experienced on the last day of school, becomes full-fledged with the

Fourth of July, begins closing down on the first day back to school, and is declared over by Labor Day weekend.

Vacations are part of our expectation of our business and personal lives. Hectic as they may be—getting ready, packing, stopping the mail, catching up when we get back—they seem to form islands of pleasure in the memories of families and individuals. After we've caught up on sleep, got laundry done and the pictures developed, how pleasing it is to sit in the restful security of home and look back on all that. I remember on the last days of a trip that took us to St. Petersburg in Russia, urging that we buy a video of St. Petersburg. Tired, my feet hurting, wondering whether we needed to spend these extra dollars on a commercial video—Hadn't I already taken eight rolls of film myself?—what made it seem such an inviting purchase was the image of my sitting on the couch, feet up on the hassock, and watching, in lovely enveloping comfort, the wonders of this city and its history unfold before me—with appropriate background music, of course.

Don't need a vacation—even if it's only a few extra days at home? I recall the story of the minister, protesting that he couldn't take a vacation (I don't know where this figure came from. I never met such a person) because, he said, "The devil never takes a vacation." To which his listener responded, "That's why he's the devil."

Summer is followed by "the busy fall season," the edging crispness of fall—Keats's "Ode to Autumn," beginning "Season of mists and mellow fruitfulness." The days grow cooler and darker and drearier. This is mercifully relieved by "the holidays," which begin with Thanksgiving and end shortly after New Year's. It is then that the darkest time of year is brightened by innumerable lights and decorations and when we are enticed into the cheery retail stores that expect to do much of their annual business during those short weeks. We visit family and friends and are generous, both to them and to the needy. We need all this cheer, for what follows is the coldest time of winter—relieved in some cultures by carnival celebrations. We often observe the New Year—in addition to partying, which is supposed to dim the pain of such an important transition—by making resolutions, many of which have slipped away by February.

Spring comes—usually too slowly to suit us—and with it our spirits brighten. New spring clothes may celebrate the warming and lengthening days. And we prepare, once again, for summer.

Families have their own seasonal rituals, occasions for refreshment. In a Sunday supplement's "Annual Family Spirit Issue" a family tells how once each year they return to what has become a family oasis for them: In the cool summer nights on the Maine coast, they light a fire in the fireplace and relax together—no homework to do, no school-night bedtimes to adhere to, the call of the loons the only sound audible. Another family tells of their annual Christmastime visit to a nearby dairy farm for scones and eggnog. My son tells me how he and his wife and two small daughters go each fall to the farm where they watch the workings of the cider press and come home with a supply of the sweet tangy juice. When our children were growing up, we would make the annual teachers' fall enrichment day (always on a Friday) the occasion for an overnight trip to one of the few remaining stands of virgin timber in our state, where we would hike the familiar trails through the tall trees and at night, cozy in our riverside cabin, play games and tell stories against the sounds of the river and the night noises of the forest. Seasonal occasions for refreshment of life.

For Christians the days and seasons of the church year, centered around the great celebrations of Easter and Christmas, are milestones that give structure and meaning to the passage of time. Each of these peak days is the focus of a cycle that begins with a preparatory season, reaches its climax in a festival season, and is followed by "ordinary time."

The highest peak of the Christian year is Easter—the day of rresurrection, new life, renewal. One cannot jump to this peak in a single leap, so it is preceded by Lent—a preparatory season of discipline and reflection upon the basics of the faith and upon one's own life. Easter itself is the last of the "Great Three Days" that begin Holy Thursday evening, when Christians retrace the journey through suffering and death to new life. Easter is also the first day of the festive Easter Season, the "Great Fifty Days" that conclude with the celebration of the spirit on the day of Pentecost. In American and European latitudes, this season coincides with spring and is mingled with the joy of lengthening and warming days. This season is followed by about six months of "ordinary time." "Ordinary" is not a put-down term; it calls to mind words like "order" and "orderly." It reflects that our journey crosses plains as well as mountain ranges.

The other peak is Christmas, which, because it falls within "the holidays," is experienced even more than Easter as a combined Christian-secular celebration. Light shines in the darkness, and hope leads to the miracle of birth. Again, it is a peak that takes time to climb, so it is preceded by the preparatory season of Advent, where, amid the busyness and pressures of getting ready for

Christmas, there is the possibility of discipline and reflection on the meaning of it all for our lives. Christmas Eve and Christmas Day begin the festive "Twelve Days of Christmas," concluding with the festival of Epiphany, also known as Three Kings Day and especially popular in the Spanish-speaking world as Día de Los Reyes. This again is followed by several weeks of "ordinary time."

At our house, we celebrate Christmas from Saint Nicholas Day to Epiphany, and we "start over" at the Jewish New Year, Chinese New Year, and the conventional New Year. Although we are neither Jewish, Chinese, nor conventional, a month without a holiday is a long month.

VICTORIA MORAN

The New Year has its own significance as a time for spiritual reflection—the Sabbath of beginning again: January 1 for those following the Gregorian calendar, variable days in winter for Chinese New Year and in the fall for Rosh Hashanah, the Jewish New Year, depending on the phases of the moon.

The Jewish Day of Atonement, in anticipation of Rosh Hashanah, is an occasion for reviewing the year, asking forgiveness for wrongdoing, and praying to become a better person. The custom of *Tashlich*, in which bread is broken into pieces and thrown into the water, is performed by Jews in some communities following Rosh Hashanah services. The bread symbolizes undesirable parts of one's self that are being discarded.

Hanukkah, the Jewish feast of lights, where oil is burned for eight days, commemorates the rededication of the temple by the Maccabees and marks the start of the dark winter.

The Jewish spring festival of Pesach celebrates the birth of a nation as it escapes from Egyptian slavery and darkness. The Passover meal commemorates that escape, made so quickly that there was no time for the bread to rise—hence the custom of serving unleavened bread at Passover, as the history of the Jewish people's emerging as a nation is celebrated through the various courses and accompanying readings from the Talmud.

The seasonal markers for Christianity and Judaism have their counterparts in the religion of Islam. Muslims date their beginnings from the *Hijra* in 622 C.E.—the flight of the Prophet Mohammed in safety from Medina to Mecca. The month of Ramadan, the month in which God revealed the Koran to the prophet Mohammed in 610 C.E., is perhaps most familiar—at least by name—to the non-Muslim world. The specter of not eating for a month is enough to draw anyone's attention. Of course Muslims eat during Ramadan, they just don't eat—or engage in sexual activity—during the hours between daylight and sunset. There are exceptions allowed to that rule, for children, the ill, and pregnant women. In most cases, the whole family eats together before sunrise and after sunset. It isn't only a shift in living patterns that is prescribed for the month of Ramadan as a way of heightening one's spiritual consciousness. Along with fasting during daylight hours, adherents are to engage in additional prayers and contemplation and a greater sharing of time and resources with the family and those in need.

In addition to the major event of Ramadan, there are other annual occasions when Muslims observe particular moments in their history. We have already alluded to Muharrem, the day marking Mohammed's migration from Mecca to Medina in 622. While this doesn't have anywhere near the scope of Ramadan with its commemoration of Mohammed's receiving the Koran, it is a day often observed by special services at the mosque. The anniversaries of the deaths of each of the Imans—the line of spiritual leaders who succeeded Mohammed—are also observed in special services.

Native Americans, particularly those descended from the plains tribes who, during the winter when game and winter berries would not provide enough food for the nation, have had to scatter across the land, now regather in a springtime Renewal and tell their stories of what has happened. The trappers, who have been huddled in their ice houses all winter, celebrate in their spring rendezvous their own form of Renewal.

Renewal is also a theme in Chinese New Year observances. A few days before the New Year, families thoroughly clean their houses in an effort to sweep away bad influences and occasions in their lives and make way for good fortune. A clean house sets the stage for a clean heart and a good year.

African-Americans observe the seven days preceding the New Year as Kwanzaa, a celebration of African-American culture. Kwanza is a Swahili word meaning "first fruits." Each day features one of the seven principles intended to bring together families, friends, and communities: unity, self-determination, collective work and responsibility, cooperative economics, purpose, creativity, and faith. The festival includes song, dance, and traditional African and African-American

A holiday is about love and lightness. Whether it is a religious, patriotic, or seasonal celebration, or some combination of these, it shouldn't take a holiday to recuperate from one. Cooking from scratch, sewing costumes, making gifts and decorations, and telling every relative you've got that there's plenty of room at your house are great if they appeal to you and if they're feasible at this time in your life. If not, make it easy on yourself by getting to know the deli manager, the nearest thrift store, a catalog, and a good motel.

VICTORIA MORAN

food. Celebrants wear African dress, decorate their homes with red, black, and green, and may exchange small gifts such as books.

The Hindu celebration of the New Year includes a day of lavish parades in which huge papier mâché sculptures in the forms of gods and monsters are paraded through the streets and accompanied with singing and chanting. This is followed by a day of reflection, during which (in countries where Hindu practice is observed) all shops are closed and people are confined to their homes under penalty of arrest if they disobey. Then the New Year can begin.

In addition to these—and other—seasonal events prescribed for the faithful, some people, knowing how easy it is for spiritual practices to become humdrum and routine, go on periodic personal retreats—perhaps to a retreat center,

> More than all things, love silence: it brings you a fruit that tongue cannot describe. In the beginning we have to force ourselves to be silent. But then there is born something that draws us to silence. May God give you an experience of this "something" that is born of silence. If you only practice this, untold LIGHT will dawn on you in consequence. . . . After a while a certain sweetness is born in the heart of this exercise and the body is drawn almost by force to remain in silence.
>
> ISAAC OF NINEVAH

or to a special place that augurs spiritual refreshment. Anne Morrow Lindbergh's classic, *Gifts from the Sea*, grew out of her search for a period of quiet contemplation.

These occasions of seasonal reprieve and refreshment may seem a far distance from our chief preoccupation here, which is how to maintain the habit of Sabbath—which we ordinarily think of as an every-seventh-day event. But these religious and cultural heritages set the larger framework in which our Sabbath observances are located and nourished.

In a different league, but perhaps equally important, are the ways in which our life patterns, day by day, nourish or discourage our ability to observe Sabbath deeply, whether it's a formal weekly occasion or a readiness to receive and honor Sabbath moments when—as the old *Candid Camera* TV show used to promise, "Somewhere, when you least expect it"—not a TV camera sprung from behind some door or post but a drift of wind, an insight that calls our name, a moment of true Sabbath blessing presents itself to us, if we have ears to hear and eyes to see. In the next pages, let's look at ways to receive and honor daily Sabbath moments.

⁓

CHAPTER TEN

The Care and Feeding of Sabbath: Daily Promptings of the Spirit

It is one thing to race or be driven by the
vicissitudes that menace life, and another
thing to stand still and to embrace the
presence of an eternal moment.

ABRAHAM JOSHUA HESCHEL

*H*ow to receive and honor daily Sabbath moments? In some ways, what is called for is a kind of reordering of life—a way of being ready for Sabbath, savoring it, living in its wake until the next time when refreshment comes. Or maybe it's a matter of taking a one-hundred-eighty-degree turn, so the same setting surrounds us but we see it differently. Or maybe it's a matter of, at least occasionally, just standing still. And noticing.

When as a young writer I submitted a poem to my college professor, acknowledging that this was very much a beginning effort and asking what I should do, she had the kindness not to comment much on the poem, but she wrote: "Try going around with your senses out on stems." That's part of it—of being ready for the daily promptings of the Spirit. Sabbath moments can come at any time, but we have to be ready to receive them.

Adopting new modes of being isn't a cure for unease of life. We'll continue to have bad times—from passing moods of "the blahs" to a sustained period of despair—what is referred to in religious literature as "the dark night of the soul." It doesn't even help a lot to know we're not alone—that even Julian of Norwich had periods of existential anxiety. I suppose Pope John Paul does, too, as does Billy Graham. It may even be that a heightened sensitivity to the moments of illumination in life makes us more aware, not less, of the vulnerabilities all around us. But we will also have a deeper and more resonant life, a sense of coherence and joy in the passing hours and days.

What are some ways to bring this about—this daily grounding in the life of the Spirit? It is an old Hasidic tradition that the first thought on waking sets the tone for the day. One is therefore enjoined to make that thought centered in the life of God. Some people use the earliest time of morning for reading, for prayer, for reflection, for anticipating the events of the day. I find, other than a brief prayer before getting up, I do better at serious thought after breakfast, and maybe even after a browse through the morning paper. In contrast, a much revered teacher advises that one move from bed to writing desk with no interruption other than perhaps a necessary stop at the bathroom—that the overhang of the dream world is as good a jumping-off place for creativity as one is likely to find. It may be so. I cannot bring myself to try it. But early morning is certainly a good time for a conscious tuning-up of the mind and spirit to be open to the events and nuances of this day.

Food has been central to religious observance—both as metaphor and as fact. The Passover meal is a pivotal event in Jewish religious life. The Eucharist, also known as the Lord's Supper or Holy Communion, is a central event in Christian worship. Feasting breaks the fast of the Muslim Ramadan.

So much more can be the acknowledged significance of food in our daily life. The Christian practice has been to offer "grace" before meals. Jewish customs include reciting prayers of blessing before a meal and prayers and singing at its conclusion. Muslims are encouraged to offer a silent prayer of thanks to God for food eaten—a custom that may require greater discipline than the before-meal version, depending on one's appraisal of the food. Which

> Watching for light was her vocation. There would be no life without light; it was the beginning; it was the substance that made things visible, that brought humanity to an awareness that cannot be seen. It could enhance a thing and make it holy.
>
> CHARLOTTE PAINTER

calls to mind my mother's account of how her father would tailor the blessing to accommodate to her sometime inability to wait properly when she was a young child: "For what we are about to receive and for what Ruth has already received, may the Lord make us truly thankful."

Our own custom when our children were small was to say together the familiar quatrain, "God is great, God is good, And we thank him for our food." As they got older we changed to holding hands and observing the Quaker custom of silent blessing. It was, we said, a way of keeping anyone from advance reaching for food, and a way of allowing for intellectual freedom as far as the contents of the blessing went. Now we sometimes join hands with small grandchildren, who take turns prompting the blessing, "God is great . . . " Only now—a welcome nod to a nonsexist view of God, the words are syntactically askew but the meaning is right. . . . "And we thank *You* for our food."

Daily family prayer was at one time an important part of family religious observance and it is still practiced in some families. The suggestions on page 78 for Sabbath family worship can be adapted, perhaps in briefer form, for daily use. Sometimes a reading—from scripture or some other special book—and a prayer for guidance and presence through the day will send everyone off with a lift. Family prayers in the evening are harder to manage with today's busy schedules. Sometimes parents will pray with young children at bedtime—a custom children may not be above exploiting, as witnessed by the father who, after repeated returns to settle his young son for sleep, came downstairs in some exasperation and said to his wife, "I told him no more praying!"

> Cultivating a spirituality for simple living involves locating and exploring those places in our soul that ring like great jubilant wind chimes . . . to the breezes and whispers of the divine. Simplicity . . . frees us from clutter so that we can wake up to and hear the great chiming within us.
>
> RICH HEFFERN

A long tradition in the Roman Catholic Church has been the Observance of the Hours. At stated periods throughout the day—and night!—the observer takes note of the hour, offers prayer for spiritual guidance. In religious communities these daily times are marked by services, where the community draws together for perhaps half an hour, to remind themselves of what they are about.

These through-the-day reminders of the spiritual roots of life can be observed in varied forms by an individual as well. A middle-aged lawyer and family man, John McQuiston II, uses his own adaptation of the sixth-century Rule of Saint Benedict, which he describes in a book, *Always We Begin Again: The Benedictine Way of Liv-*

ing, which has become its publisher's best-seller. He tells how he was looking not for another creed but for a way to get through the days while remaining mindful of the Big Picture. His solution—his adaptation of the Benedictine rule, which he came upon after the death of his father and which struck him as a sane marriage of faith and daily life—includes knitting bits of time for meditation into his sometimes frantic routine: Give thanks seven times each day. Breathe deeply when tense. Slow down. Share with the family. Other guiding principles: "Live this life, and do whatever is done in a spirit of thanksgiving. Abandon attempts to achieve security; they are futile. Give up the search for wealth; it is demeaning. Quit the search for salvation; it is selfish. And come to comfortable rest in the certainty that those who participate in this life with an attitude of thanksgiving will receive its full promise." He proposes a weekday schedule:

6:45–7:15 A.M. Reading and meditation. Meditate in the same place each day. Be thankful.

Breakfast. Share this time with a family member, if possible. If not, read something helpful.

Work. Slow down when you feel yourself racing. The world does not depend upon you.

Lunch. Eat with friends if possible. Take time to live and share.

2:30–2:31 P.M. Say a quiet thanksgiving.

Postwork family time. Turn off the TV and discover how much more time you have in a single evening.

10–10:10 P.M. Give thanksgiving. Skip the evening news and discover that the life you are leading is not full of violence and tragedy.

Of his rule, he says, "You can change your habits in the path of life. I'm much less anxious about things. You can learn trust—telling the truth in the courtroom and to everybody and trusting it will all work out." A good way of making the most of each day.

The Muslim custom of *salat*, in which worshipers face toward Mecca and recite formal ritual prayers at dawn, noon, afternoon, sunset, and late evening, keeps Muslims in daily touch with their tradition. These prayers may be offered in assembled groups or by individuals wherever they are at these appointed hours. Sometimes the more hectic the life, the more necessary become these periods for restoring perspective. In an article, "Quest to Satisfy the Soul" in the San Jose Mercury News, Richard Scheiner writes of Muslim Hisham Abdallah, a clinical pharmacologist in California. Abdallah describes the maze and pressure of his work life, and his urgent need for moments of peace: "I'll be in the middle of all these meetings, dealing with so many people, and waiting for the time to close my door, spread my prayer rug on the floor and pray to God." Devout Shiite Muslims are encouraged to carry with them a small molded block of clay from the site of the great martyrdoms, so that when they prostrate themselves for prayer their foreheads will touch the soil of Kaba, a huge black stone in the House of God at Mecca.

Among Christians a common lectionary, in which particular scripture passages are suggested for each day's reading, is widely used. Many devotional books are designed for daily reading—a way of "warming up" the spiritual muscles for the day.

Personal prayers—of gratitude, of petition, for centering—mark the daily life of many believers. One way of helping to focus the spirit is to arrange a private prayer center. I once attended an exhibit of individual women's "prayer centers." Each woman had assembled cherished and evocative objects and arranged them on a table or shelf. The arrangements were very personal to their creator—perhaps a piece of driftwood, some dried flowers, a small photograph, a poem, a book, a string of amber beads. The use of icons—stylized paintings of saints and biblical scenes—in meditation is seen by some as a way of getting in touch with the eternal. One looks *through* these pictures (they often have mesmerizing eyes), not *at* them, and perhaps the worlds of time and eternity, of spirit and matter, of the divine and the human will meld into a sense of mutual presence, of touching the eternal.

In any attempt to invoke the Spirit through tangible objects there is almost always a candle. The importance of light, the many associations we have with light—"Let there be light, and there was light" (Genesis 1:3). An old Quaker axiom counsels "It is better to light a candle than to curse the darkness." The festivals of light as the Earth darkens.

And so we light candles.

One writer tells how, wherever she is, she lights a candle before she starts her day's work. Then invokes the Spirit of the muse, releases herself from worry and preoccupying care, affirms her own being in the world, pauses to let the silence enter in and spread to her fingertips. Others tell of closing the day with a similar ritual of relinquishment.

Transcendental Meditation, the different forms of yoga, the Relaxation Response—all help through breathing, imagery, and, in the case of yoga, through assumed postures and exercises to set and sustain the tone of the day, as well as encourage improved bodily health and mobility, and create the scene where Sabbath moments can alight. Herbert Benson, the Harvard-based cardiologist and author of two best-selling books, *The Relaxation Response* and *Timeless Healing*, describes the ideal health-care model as a three-legged stool, made up of pharmaceuticals, surgery, and self-care. In his work at Harvard's Mind/Body Institute, which he founded in 1988, he and his colleagues discovered that the people who were best able to invoke the Relaxation Response—which has been proven to significantly reduce the damaging effects of stress—regularly claimed to feel more spiritual, which manifested itself in two ways: "One was the feeling of a presence of a power, a force, an energy—God. Secondarily, that presence was close to them."

> The Buddhists refer to meditation with a charming understatement. They call it "sitting." . . . We tend to think of sitting only as the favored pose of the unmotivated and uninspired, staring at TV screens or playing electronic games until their bodies and minds resemble cornmeal mush that should have been cooked longer. But this indictment of sitting is unfair. There is a time, to paraphrase Satchel Paige, to "sometimes sit and think—and sometimes to just sit."
>
> VICTORIA MORAN

Do we not have time? As the pharmacologist in Silicon Valley said, the busier we are, the more we need to allow ourselves breathing room.

Books, magazines, newspapers everywhere offer guidelines to help us, and testimonies to the value of living with intention, of not allowing ourselves to become captive to frenzied activity, of preserving not only the weekly Sabbath but the sustaining qualities of Sabbath throughout our lives.

A few quick clues. Find your own formula. A friend who was a busy editor in New York tells how he accustomed himself to not wearing a watch as a symbol of free-ing himself from the tyranny of time. On certain types of retreats one of the first instructions to retreatants is to put away their watches.

Other life disciplines? Anything that promotes good health. Getting enough exercise, and enough sleep. Eating healthily. It is dismaying to learn of the high and growing proportion of Americans—including children and young people—who are clinically obese.

We each have to find our own way. In the quiet times (first prerequisite: Make space for quiet times) and with paper and pencil in hand, make a list of what you value most in life. Then ask some questions, for example:

How does my present life conform to this list?

Are there things I can't change?

Are there things I can change? How?

Is there some way to ameliorate the negative attri-butes of the things I can't change?

Are there occasions in my life the way it is structured now that I could make better use of?

Another area for consideration: How do you use your waiting time? Do you spend precious moments waiting for a phone call? Waiting for someone to pick you up? Waiting for it to stop snowing or for the cake to come out of the oven? Instead of inwardly spinning wheels of frus-tration, try taking a few slow deep breaths, letting mind and body and spirit coalesce in a moment of stillness in an otherwise busy day. It is quite possible the irritating aspects of the situation will diminish if not disappear.

There is another kind of waiting, which is really not waiting as much as it is stepping out of the expected stream of life to honor an inner prompting. In a moving article in *The New Yorker*, "Fall from Grace: How modern life has made waiting a desperate act," Noelle Oxenhandler writes of feeling a compulsion in anticipation of giving birth to go and lie on the beach for awhile. She tells of a child who, when she was five years old, was told she was adopted, and had been born to other parents. The adoptive father recounts, " 'She didn't cry. She didn't say a word. She went into our bedroom. She climbed onto our bed and curled up at the foot of it. She lay there, in fetal position, for an entire afternoon.' " Oxenhandler goes on to say that she has always remembered the story and the sureness with which the child took care of herself. The child had to leave the "linear movement of time and take her place inside a different rhythm." Surely a time of Sabbath for this child—and for the adoptive parents who had the wisdom to stand away and let her make the journey only she could make. A painful time, a holy time of resolution. In the end, a Sabbath time.

> Holy leisure is not for the asking, but for the loving. It demands unity. It listens for God.
>
> VERNON SCHMID

Oxenhandler contrasts these stories of taking time to respond to urgent interior voices with the modern obsession—and capability, now that it is possible to fax a message from New York to Bangkok in minutes—of charging on, attending to tasks. The commuter who clicks away at his laptop while the blazing autumn color outside the train window goes unnoticed. The writer who has lost that lovely respite of several days while the manuscript, at last completed, goes through the mail because the fax machine will get it there and back—with needed revisions suggested—before there's time for a celebratory dinner and a good night's sleep. These are the moments—and hours—we need to lay claim to and preserve. These are the moments—and hours—of Sabbath time.

Testimony abounds to the value of making significant changes in one's life in order to make room for the life of the spirit.

In a Sunday issue of *USA Week-end*, families share ways in which they structure their lives to allow for more flowering of the Spirit. A

> In returning and rest you shall be saved. In quietness and in trust shall be your strength.
>
> ISAIAH 30:15

father of six children tells how once a year he takes each of his children out to lunch—just the two of them. Another family tells how they make space in their lives for the telling of family stories.

Family stories. I recall stories my mother told about visiting her extended family in England—even to the sorry tale of the unpleasant neighbor child whom some relative kept inviting to the house so my mother, who would have much preferred the company of the grown-ups "would have somebody to play with," and her recall of her mother's stories of going out with her university student brother to hear him recite his lessons to her as they walked over "Rounds Green Hills" peopled my imagination. When I had occasion to go to the town in England from which my grandmother emigrated as a young woman, I asked a kindly woman who was showing us around the churchyard if there was still a place known as "Rounds Green Hills." She turned and pointed to the rise of green slopes behind us. "Right there," she said, and I was startled to feel tears of recognition spring to my eyes. When I return to the New England city in which I—and my father before me—grew up, and pass a particular grove of trees in a low valley near my father's boyhood home, I recall his account of how during the spring, as a young boy regaining strength after typhoid fever but unable to go to school yet, he would walk down into that grove, vestiges of snow still on the ground, and watch maple sap drip into the buckets his father had hung from the trees. And I see him there—a gentle, contemplative boy, keenly attentive to nature—precursor of the man he would become. Family stories. Mini-sabbaths along the way. Occasions for refreshment of life.

Other clues to improving the quality of our life, so that we make room for a "Sabbath mentality" to find us—on our weekend day of Sabbath and at other graced moments of our lives? Articles and books—some serious, some light-hearted—appear frequently in magazines and newspapers and on the shelves of bookstores, extolling the simplification of life and the return to a day of quietude, or at least to a day that is intentionally *different* from our busy, often frazzled days. Herewith some sample advice:

"Enumerate your roles, according to which are most important and which take up most time; synchronize the lists according to your own priorities." Andrea Steenhouse, *A WOMAN'S GUIDE TO A SIMPLER LIFE.*

"Exercise; Laugh or Smile; Pray; Avoid Caffeine; Eat Sweets (but stay away from chocolate—high in caffeine); Take a Warm Bath; Rock On—Rocking Motions are not just for infants. Beverly Potter, *THE WORRYWART'S COMPANION.*

"Meditation. Set your own agenda. Focus on work tasks one at a time. Try focusing at home, too. Turn off the television." Janet Iris Sussman, *TIMESHIFT: The Experience of Dimensional Change.*

"Take a look at how you define success. Learn to plan.

Learn to say no. Resolve ongoing conflict. Play hard." And my favorite: "Stop being impatient. Now." Dianna Booher, *GET A LIFE WITHOUT SACRIFING YOUR CAREER.*

The preservation of Sabbath as a holy day is being welcomed anew as an inviting life choice. Victoria Moran, in *SHELTER FOR THE SPIRIT*, writes, "Now that we can buy anything we like on Sunday . . . there is an increasing trend toward refraining from doing so. I meet more and more people as I travel who keep Sunday—or Saturday or Friday depending upon religious background and personal inclination—a day apart." She tells of a speaker at a conference who acknowledged his reluctance to be doing this on a Saturday because it had become his custom, as part of his Jewish faith, to keep Saturday for reverence and reflection. "As he spoke, the room was so quiet you could have heard someone else's conscience. In a diverse and largely secular audience, he had struck a chord."

Probably many of us recall the movie, *Chariots of Fire,* is based on the life of Eric Lindell, the Olympic runner, and how he refused to participate in a key race because it was being run on Sunday. His refusal cost him the race, but he was at peace with himself.

So, we have come full circle. An honored weekly Sabbath observance. And a readiness, fed by this weekly observance, to recognize the Sabbath quality in random moments of our lives.

The reciprocity of weekly Sabbath observance and a pervasive readiness to find Sabbath occasions throughout the week is probably hard to overestimate. I think of the children's playground seesaw, or teeter-totter as we used to call it, and of how the motion of the child on one end is dependent on the rhythmic rise and fall on the other end.

All apart from the seesaw, children can teach us much about living in the moment. It is no effort for them—that is how they conduct their lives. "Are you God?" a questioner asks the Buddha. "No, I am awake," the Buddha responds. To simplify our lives, get our priorities in order, is to allow for the moments of searching awareness to come to full blossom, is to live in a remembrance of the garden and the promise of returning again to our Maker—at the end of our lives, to be sure. But in the meantime, while we play out our yearning for illumination and peace, for growth and a sense of "arrival" in the key moments and relationships, of work and play, we can come home again to the Sabbath, sometimes on off moments when we least expect it, but always in the knowledge that, week by week, regular as clockwork and the motion of planets through the sky and the turning of the Earth, we can return to Sabbath one day each week, and be made whole.

Better is a handful with quiet than two handfuls with toil and a chasing after wind.

ECCLESIASTES 4:6

CHAPTER ELEVEN

52+ Ways to Honor the Sabbath

*H*ere, to spur you on your way, are some suggestions—some lighthearted, some mightily serious, on how you might observe, or evoke, Sabbath. Read them with a pencil in hand. In the spaces between the suggestions, jot down phrases or words—or spin-offs—that come to mind that could enrich this activity. Put a star beside those you think you might try. Then add some of your own.

1. Take a book you loved as a child to a nearby park—or your own yard—and spend an hour or two letting its meaning and associations come to you again.

2. Spend some time lying on a hammock or a blanket and looking up at the trees. Imagine the sounds of the trees are speaking to you. What are they saying?

3. Rent a video of a favorite movie—or one you've wanted to see but haven't taken the time for yet. Some suggestions: *Singin' in the Rain, Babette's Feast, Places of the Heart.*

4. Take a leisurely, warm bath—with candles and incense if you like. Pay attention to the qualities and gifts of water, its place in our lives.

5. Offer to take someone "without wheels" for a drive. Stop somewhere and get an ice-cream cone.

6. Go to church, synagogue, temple, or mosque of your choice, making a conscious effort to leave your pre-occupations at home and be present to the unfolding meanings of the service.

7. If you live near a desert—or some sand dunes—where you can find a quiet spot, take a folding chair or a blanket and spend an hour or two, observing the play of the wind, the small creatures who live out their lives there. (If you are by an ocean, the sea will be a constant in your awareness.)

8. Unplug the phone and take the battery out of your beeper. Then ask yourself, "What do I most want to do with this day?" If it's to reconnect the phone and call someone . . . go ahead and do it, but wait awhile first.

9. Write a letter you've not made time for during the week. May Sarton, according to a biographer, had a life-long habit of spending Sunday morning at her desk writing letters in what she called "my Sunday religious service, devoted to friendship."

10. Sit in a comfortable chair, close your eyes, and fantasize all the tension in your body flowing like sand out through your fingers and toes. After awhile (if you've not gone to sleep), open your eyes and let your eyes linger on the familiar objects around you.

11. Give yourself permission to read, read, read—but nothing connected with work.

12. Make a long-distance call to someone you've been wanting to refresh your acquaintance with, but have kept putting it off.

13. Attend a church, synagogue, temple, or mosque of your choice. Take with you a small photograph of someone you love, tucked into a pocket.

14. Stay in bed all day, getting up to fix yourself a tray of wonderful goodies. Read some poetry. If you have a partner, read aloud to each other.

15. Take some time to dwell on the context of this day. Reflect on the recent past, what you see forthcoming in the year ahead. Drop a plumb line from this day, down through the years as you remember events from the past. What was going on on this day a year ago? Five years? Ten?

16. Read a religious text from another faith. What might it be like to be an adherent of that faith? Think of your friends and acquaintances who may follow another faith. Hold these persons in your heart, as a blessing.

17. Offer to bring dinner to someone for whom food preparation is hard. Depending on your sense of that person's preference, offer to stay and eat with him or her, or leave with a gracious smile, a handshake, or a hug.

18. Gather your own "company of saints" around you—people you love who are far away or who have died. Write down the names of these persons, assemble photos if you have them. Relish their presence. Introduce them to each other. What would they say?

19. Pack a lunch and go for an all-day walk—or bike ride—or drive (unless your Sabbath observance precludes that). If you have a destination in mind, fine. If not, "go where your feet take you."

20. Go to church, synagogue, temple, or mosque. If your church has two services, try the one you don't usually attend. Or go to both!

21. Go to a museum, or a zoo, or a library. Look around at the people there. Wish them well.

22. Go with a child on an outing to the park or some other place where you can lie back and watch the cloud formations overhead. Tell each other what you see in those clouds.

23. Go for a walk with someone you love—perhaps to some quiet, woodsy place. Or if you're in the city, walk with particular attention to the architecture and building use of the places you pass. What would it be like to work/live there?

24. Look through the Sunday paper for listings of available courses coming up. Imagine yourself signing up for one of them—maybe an art course, or a foreign language course? Make a note of time, phone number, etc., and plan to make a phone call tomorrow.

25. Pray. If you're not accustomed to praying, close your eyes, breathe slowly and deeply, and conjure up a favorite image—the ocean, a hallowed spot in your own history, a candle, a face. Stay in that image's presence for some minutes. Sense the power in that association. Remember the words of Wallace Stevens: "God and the imagination are one." Or these words of Helen Keller: "I believe that God is in me as the sun is in the color and fragrance of a flower—the Light in my darkness, the voice in my silence."

26. Borrow or buy a "children's toy"—a book of paper dolls, a simple model airplane kit, a set of magnets—and play with it. You might want a child to share this with you—or do it by yourself!

27. Invite someone to go with you—to the church, synagogue, temple, or mosque of your choice. Or arrange to meet with someone after service and go out to a meal together.

28. Take a notebook and pen and write down whatever comes to mind—rambling thoughts, phrases, the view you have from where you sit. Write five reasons to be glad for this day, this time.

29. Clean a closet. This is dangerously close to work; don't do it on the Sabbath unless it seems prospectively fun, a genuine choice for freedom, an opportunity to "unclutter" your life.

30. Gather with friends for a festive meal together. Tell family stories about how each of you used to observe (or try to bypass) the Sabbath.

31. Make this a "touching" day, to savor the textures of the earth. Go barefoot on the grass if you can. Run your hand over the textures of fabric, of tree trunks, of your own skin.

32. Go to a concert, or listen to a favorite CD or tape.

33. Tonight, after dark, go outside and listen to the sounds of night.

34. Attend church, synagogue, temple, or mosque. As you are seated, if the service has not yet begun, pick up the service book or hymnal and, holding it in your hand, imagine all the people who, before you, have held this book as part of their worship here.

35. Make a point today to eat very slowly, savoring each bite of food. Especially if you tend to overeat or eat impulsively, pause frequently to ask yourself, "Am I still hungry? Is this a good place to stop?"

36. Volunteer to work at a soup kitchen for part of the day. For the remainder of the day, rest and reflect on the soup kitchen experience.

37. Take a pair of binoculars to the park and watch birds. If there are children playing in the park, it's okay to focus on them from time to time, to enjoy their spontaneity and see what they're up to.

38. Get some seeds or cuttings and plant a small herb garden to put in a window box—or in the ground if you have access to ground for planting.

39. Cook some exotic item you've enjoyed eating but never have gone to the trouble to prepare yourself.

40. If there's a nearby lake, consider going fishing. Or just go out in a boat—maybe with a book—and sit. Isn't this half the value of fishing anyway?

41. Plan a special breakfast, being grateful for food— before going to the church, synagogue, temple, or mosque of your choice.

42. Take a kite—and some children if you can—to a vacant field and fly kites.

43. Prune your houseplants. Add potting soil if they need it. Talk to them. It may or may not encourage their growth, but it will do nice things for you.

44. Visit an aquarium. Take a child with you if you can. Consider getting a fish tank for your home. Decide not to—something else to take care of.

45. Catch up with your journal or diary. If you're already caught up, go back and read some of the earlier pages.

46. Get out some travel folders or guidebooks and think about where you'd like to go. Imagine the trip—the travel, what you might see, the new friends you might make. Look up one or two of the most significant spots in an encyclopedia. Then decide (usually) that "armchair travel" is the best kind—a lot less tiring, and a lot less expensive. But, once in a while, go.

47. On your way to the church, synagogue, temple, or mosque of your choice, sing some of the songs of the faith—in a loud voice. If other family members are with you, encourage them to join in. Or at least tell them what you're doing.

48. Go for a swim. Swim vigorously for a while. Then turn over on your back and just let the water take you where it will. (This is easier to manage in a natural body of water than in a community pool, where you are likely to create a traffic hazard if you're too relaxed about where you're going.)

49. Get a coloring book and a box of crayons and have fun. You don't have to "stay within the lines," but you probably will.

50. Make out an extra check (beyond your usual pledge if you have one) to put in the offering when you attend the church, synagogue, temple, or mosque of your choice. Mark it for some discretionary fund that will go to someone who comes in desperate need of help.

51. Light a fire in the fireplace and curl up with a book, or a partner, and enjoy the fire.

52. Look through some old family photo albums. Call up one of the people whose pictures you see and tell him or her what you're doing: "I was just looking through some old photo albums. Remember that time when we . . . "

53. Find a porch swing. Sit on it and let your foot guide you to a gentle swaying ride.

SPARES

Get on a swing (test it to support a grown-up's weight) and pump yourself as high as you can go.

Experiment with ways of praying: Sitting quietly trying to think of nothing. If that doesn't work, choose a key word (light, presence, infinite) and say that silently over and over. "Hold in the light" a succession of people you love. Include yourself.

Sing lullabies to yourself, cradling your arms against your body and swaying your shoulders gently back and forth.

Get some clay or Play-Doh and let your hands play with it. Think of James Weldon Johnson's image of God, reaching down to gather a ball of clay and creating a world.

⌐Make yourself a lovely cup of tea. Arrange some orange slices and several light cookies on a plate. Take them out onto the porch and enjoy them as you watch people passing by.

⌐Go to a worship service of a different denomination or faith. Go in the expectation of finding something that will feed your soul, challenge your imagination.

⌐Scatter incense around your house. If you don't have any on hand, put a few grains of cinnamon on the stove in a piece of foil and turn the light on very low until the scent permeates the room. (Don't forget to turn off the stove!)

⌐In a quiet setting, recall some past event that was filled with some special gift or special challenge. Try to reimagine yourself back into that event. At the time—or now, as you reflect on it—did you have any sense of a special presence being part of that for you? How does that seem now? Acknowledge, perhaps with a prayer of gratitude, the special place that event has had in your development and self-understanding.

Go to a quiet place, pen and paper in hand, and make a list of all the aspects of your life you're grateful for right now. Take a few moments to dwell on each one.

CHAPTER TWELVE

A Brief Word about the Eighth Day of Creation

The eighth day? Is this another attempt to reshape the calendar?

No.

Well, what is it then?

The eighth day is the day after the Sabbath.

Is that Sunday or Monday? And why the eighth day? Don't we start over with days one to seven?

The eighth day is the day after the Sabbath—Sunday, if one observes the Sabbath on Saturday; Monday, if one observes Sunday as Sabbath.

Mm-hmm. Thanks a lot.

To an outsider, the phrase "the eighth day" must sound like a kind of illusory doublespeak. Even to an insider it can be confusing. But the phrase comes up and calls for a brief explanation.

The eighth day is more an abstract concept than a specific twenty-four-hour day. It refers to the day after Sabbath, be that Saturday or Sunday when, refreshed and remotivated by the blessedness of Sabbath, we are ready to engage the world in fresh beginnings. The concept of a paradisal eighth day comes from Jewish thought and took on a new meaning for Christians, who considered Jesus'

Good Sabbaths make good societies.

DOROTHY BASS

resurrection on the Sabbath so life-giving as to render all time after that a new creation. Patristic tradition speaks about Sunday as the eighth or last day, a continuation and fulfillment of the Sabbath. It is seen as "a day which should last forever."

But in the meantime, the Sabbath calls to us, hallowing our days, casting its blessings over all of our lives, for all of our life.

Bibliography

alive now! Nashville: *The Upper Room*, July/August 1989.

Bass, Dorothy C., ed. *Practicing Our Faith*. San Francisco: Jossey-Bass, 1997.

Bateson, Mary Catherine. *Peripheral Visions*. New York: HarperCollins, 1994.

Benson, Herbert. *Timeless Healing*. New York: Scribner's, 1996.

Berry, Wendell. *Sabbaths*. San Francisco: North Point Press, 1987.

Dawn, Marva J. *Keeping the Sabbath Wholly*. Grand Rapids: William B. Eerdmans, 1989.

Edwards, Tilden. *Sabbath Time*. Nashville: Upper Room Books, 1992.

Friends of Silence. Jericho, Vermont. December 1996.

Hanh, Thich Nhat. The Miracle of Mindfulness. Boston: Beacon Press, 1992.

Heschel, Abraham Joshua. The Sabbath. New York: Farrar, Straus and Giroux, 1951.

Hickman, Hoyt L., Don E. Saliers, Laurence Hull Stookey, James F. White. *The New Handbook of the Christian Year*. Nashville: Abingdon Press, 1986, 1992.

Hickman, Hoyt L. *A Primer for Church Worship*. Nashville: Abingdon Press, 1984.

Liturgy, vol. 20, no. 10., Washington: The Liturgical Conference, December, 1975.

Martin, Earl. Untitled article in *TREK*. Akron: Mennonite Central Committee, July/August 1997.

McQuiston II, John. *Always We Begin Again: The Benedictine Way of Living*. Harrisburg: Morehouse Publishing, 1996.

Metford, J. C. J. *The Christian Year*. New York: Crossroad, 1991.

Moran, Victoria. *Shelter for the Spirit*. New York: Harper-Collins, 1997.

Nanji, Azim A., ed. *The Muslim Almanac*. Detroit: Gale Research Inc., 1996.

New Revised Standard Version Bible. Nashville, Thomas Nelson, 1989.

Oxenhandler, Noelle. "Fall from Grace." *The New Yorker.* New York, June 16, 1997.

Scheinin, Richard. "Quest to Satisfy the Soul." In *San Jose Mercury News*. San Jose, October 2, 1996.

Sleeth, Natalie. "Come! Come! Everybody Worship!" Nashville: Cokesbury, 1991.

Speight, R. Marston. *God is One: the Way of Islam*. New York: Friendship Press, 1989.

Stookey, Laurence Hull. *Calendar: Christ's Time for the Church.* Nashville: Abingdon Press, 1996.

Symposium: The Reader in the Electronic Age. New York: *Authors Guild Bulletin*, Winter, 1997.

USA Weekend. 9th Annual Family Spirit Issue. Arlington, Nov. 22-24, 1996.

Ward, Benedicta, trans. *The Sayings of the Desert Fathers.* Kalamazoo: Cistercian Publications, 1975.

Zerubavel, Eviatar. *The Seven Day Circle*. New York: The Free Press, 1985.

Permissions

Grateful acknowledgment is given for permission to reprint from the following:

Excerpts from *Practicing Our Faith*, Dorothy C. Bass, Editor. Copyright © 1997 by Jossey-Bass. Published by Jossey-Bass Publishers, San Francisco. Reprinted by permission.

Wendell Berry, "I go among trees and sit still" and "Whatever is foreseen in joy." From *Sabbaths* by Wendell Berry. Copyright © 1987 by Wendell Berry. Published by North Point Press. Reprinted by permission.

Ciferni, Andrew D. "Making A Day Holy." Published in *Liturgy*, December, 1975. The Liturgical Conference, 8750 Georgia Avenue, Suite 123, Silver Spring, MD 20910-3621. All rights reserved. Reprinted with permission.

Excerpt from *KEEPING THE SABBATH WHOLLY* by Marva J. Dawn. Copyright © 1989 by William B. Eerdmans Publishing Co. Reprinted by permission.

Excerpts from *SABBATH TIME* by Tilden Edwards. Copyright © 1992 by Tilden Edwards. Reprinted by permission of Upper Room Books. (Toll free order at 1-800-972-0433)

Excerpts from *THE SABBATH* by Abraham Joshua Heschel. Copyright © 1951 by Abraham Joshua Heschel, copyright renewed 1979 by Sylvia Heschel. Published by Farrar, Straus and Giroux. First Noonday Press paperback edition, 1975. Reprinted by permission.

"Soup Kitchen Sabbath" by Dee Word Horn. Published in *alive now!* July/August 1989. Copyright © 1989 by *alive now!* Reprinted by permission of the author.

Excerpt from "Right of Leavetaking" by Robert Hovda. Published in *Liturgy*, December 1975. The Liturgical Conference, 8750 Georgia Avenue, Suite 123, Silver Spring, MD 20910-3621. All rights reserved. Reprinted with permission.